CONSPIRACY AMONG AMERICA'S HEROES

Chief Kelly Daugherty, MS, EFO, CFO, MIFireE

authorHOUSE®

AuthorHouse™
1663 Liberty Drive
Bloomington, IN 47403
www.authorhouse.com
Phone: 1-800-839-8640

Published by AuthorHouse   9/13/12

ISBN: 978-1-4772-6868-1 (sc)
ISBN: 978-1-4772-6867-4 (dj)
ISBN: 978-1-4772-6866-7 (e)

Library of Congress Control Number: 2012917283

Any people depicted in stock imagery provided by Thinkstock are models, and such images are being used for illustrative purposes only. Certain stock imagery © Thinkstock.

This book is printed on acid-free paper.

This book is dedicated to all those who believe in doing the right thing—every time, without reservation, regardless of political or peer pressure.

Portions of the book's proceeds will be donated to the National Fallen Firefighters Foundation, Emmitsburg, Maryland, in honor of those who strove to make a difference and have perished in the process.

An exceptional "tip of the helmet" is hereby extended to the following organizations for granting me permission to utilize portions of their material:

"Fire Chief under Attack," International Association of Fire Chiefs

"The Fire Service Reputation Management White Paper,"

Cumberland Valley Volunteer Firemen's Association

"Adverse to Vision," *Fire Chief* magazine

"The Psychology of Living a Lie," *Dr. Gail Saltz, MD.*

"Keeping Your Lens Clean Amidst Ethical Challenges," *Public Manager* magazine

This is a true story. The name of the jurisdiction(s) and individual(s) involved were changed. It is my hope that by presenting the unethical and iniquitous behaviors I experienced would help other fire service leaders guide their organizations through troubling waters.

This book was made possible by the unwavering support of my wife, our sons, their wives, my parents, and friends throughout the United States of America.

Contents

Reckless Conduct Endangers the American Fire Service

"What does not destroy me makes me strong."
—*Friedrich Nietzsche*

According to the International Association of Fire Chiefs (IAFC), the publication, *Fire Chief under Attack* states that over the past few years, progressive and respected fire chiefs across the country have become victims of coordinated and well-planned attacks by labor unions.

The trend of attacking the fire chief is on the rise. Now the International Association of Fire Chiefs is doing something about it. They have developed an effective program to educate chiefs about the circumstances surrounding these attacks, how to avoid conflicts, and how to respond appropriately when attacks do occur. IAFC members, who were viciously attacked by their unions wrote the booklet, *Fire Chief under Attack*.

Their families were affected, and their careers were jeopardized. Some of them lost their jobs. By describing what can happen, we hope to help you avoid such conflicts. Chief Gary L. Nichole, past IAFC president, states that each of us deserves a level playing field. However, when the playing field becomes a mountain, the IAFC and its headquarters staff stand ready to assist you.

Hagerstown, Maryland, March 10, 2010: Reckless and inappropriate conduct by a small minority of the nation's fire service is eroding the high moral ground occupied by firefighters, says a white paper sponsored by the Cumberland Valley Volunteer Firemen's Association, (CVVFA).

The contents of the white paper represent a distillation of several fire service leadership meetings that identified a series of social, cultural, and ethical issues influencing the fire service nationwide that demand increased awareness. The white paper is intended as a wake-up call to the fire service.

The detrimental impact from fire service members who engage in unethical, immoral, inappropriate, criminal, or other activities reflects back not just to these individuals but also to their departments and communities—and to the fire service as a whole.

Recognizing that the actions of a small minority of unscrupulous individuals can have grievous widespread consequences, the fire service as a whole must be increasingly vigilant in policing itself. Through a combination of enhanced and improved internal controls, increased vigilance, and greater acceptance of personal responsibility perhaps including but not limited to abiding by a code of ethics, the fire service can ensure that it remains true to its roots and heritage of protecting and serving this great nation.

The Fire Service Reputation Management white paper clearly identifies these individuals and behaviors in a clear and cogent manner, articulates some excellent solutions, and clamors for a code of ethics as the next logical step for our profession. "We may never have the opportunity again, and I urge all fire service leaders to develop, establish, disseminate, abide, and enforce a Fire Service Code of Ethics," said Kelvin Cochran, past United States fire administrator. It is up to us to make the right choices.

CHAPTER 1
Things Mom Never Told You

*"Insanity is doing the same thing over and
over and expecting a different result."*
—*Albert Einstein*

Have you ever experienced things that you were never taught you would encounter? Remember taking your driver's license practical examination and not being told by your mother or father that the examiner would be hovering over you like a bald eagle scoping out his prey? How about when you first started school, not realizing that there were other students eyeing your lunch pail?

What about when you went on your first date—scared as ever, not knowing what to expect, when your date gives you a little peck on the lips? As time progressed, you found yourself falling in love and then, after some inexplicable event—you found yourself breaking up with the person you had come to love and appreciate!

We all know that "breaking up is hard to do" is an understatement. Breaking up can be compared to experiencing the death of someone close. It is an emotional and physical experience. You have lost someone who is very important to you. Your thoughts still dwell on them throughout the day. They were a major part of your dreams and your thoughts of the future. That is all gone now, and you feel empty. Physically you feel hungry, but food will not help.

The hardest part is that you now have to think in a completely new way, and your mind refuses to cooperate. Your thought patterns are ingrained into thinking about life in reference to your ex. You have no idea what to do next; your life ahead seems foggy, and you are a bit scared. Your thoughts, fed by your emotions, consider the situation and make you want to call your ex, explain yourself, do anything just to get back together.

However, contacting your ex is the wrong thing to do at this time in the breakup. You need a unique and well-thought-out approach to relationships and specifically getting back together with your ex. You need an overall plan and techniques that can overcome even the most challenging obstacles to making up. If you are in a relationship that has hit a rough spot, or you have already broken up and really want your ex back, then you need an overall plan, not just "tricks" to manipulate the other person into doing what you want.

These are some of life's unknown moments. Some act as precursors for future life events, like the excitement you feel when your team wins the big football game or when your firstborn child brings love into your life. These are breathtaking events that you can carry throughout your life.

In the business world, there are people who are out to make life miserable for you. These individuals have a mission: to get you to follow their guiding principles of laziness, misrepresentation, and deception, while you are struggling to convince them that their way of thinking is counterproductive to a healthy business environment.

In our lives, we experience deception, betrayal, and grievances. We feel anger, hatred, and pain. It sometimes seems that we cannot trust anybody. So many crazy people out there and a world full of lies. Just look at the amount of crime being committed. How can people act this way? Are we being victimized? Could we forgive those who trespass against us? If they do 90 percent good things but 10 percent bad things, could we just forgive them?

Individuals who seek self-satisfaction often engage in unethical, inappropriate behavior to "get back" at those who placed "undue burdens" upon them. This is often labeled as workplace revenge or organizational vengeance.

These "campaigners" engage in general action and purposeful retaliation within the workplace, in an attempt to seek what they feel is justice. The retaliator views acts of revenge in the workplace as a defensive act in response to the offender's unwarranted and unfair actions. When the offender makes the first move that is viewed by an affected colleague as unjust, the victim will often feel a need for retaliation.

Employees who engage in acts of workplace revenge are unprofessional and out-of-control individuals seeking serious vengeance against the company or a person. They also feel that they are victims of interpersonal conflicts within the organization who are compelled to seek justice by their own means—illegal or unethical as the case may be.

This revenge behavior often leads to workplace bullying. This is a tendency by individuals or groups to use persistent aggressive or unreasonable behavior against a coworker, subordinate, or employer. Workplace bullying can include such tactics as verbal, nonverbal, psychological, or physical abuse and humiliation.

This type of aggression is particularly difficult because, unlike typical forms of school bullying, workplace bullies often manipulate while operating within certain boundaries. Bullying in the workplace, whether perpetrated by management or employees, takes a wide variety of forms. Bullying can be covert or overt.

I learned that even though I have earned a number of college degrees, no classroom teaches the negative behaviors of others. You must experience them firsthand. As I travel through life, I have learned a few things:

- Life is not fair, but it is still good.
- You do not have to win every argument. Agree to disagree.
- It is okay to get angry with God. He can take it.
- Do not compare your life to others'. You have no idea what their journey is all about.
- If a relationship has to be a secret, you should not be in it.
- Everything can change in the blink of an eye. Nevertheless, do not worry; God never blinks.
- Take a deep breath. It calms the mind.
- Whatever does not kill you really does make you stronger.
- It is never too late to have a happy childhood. However, the second one is up to you and no one else.
- When it comes to going after what you love in life, do not take *no* for an answer.
- Burn the candles, and use the nice sheets. Do not save things for a special occasion. Today is special.
- Overprepare and then go with the flow.
- Be eccentric now. Do not wait for old age to wear purple.
- The most important organ is the brain.
- No one is in charge of your happiness except you.
- What other people think of you is none of your business.

- Time heals almost everything. Give time, time.
- However good or bad a situation is—it will change.
- Your job will not take care of you when you are sick. Your friends will. Stay in touch.
- Believe in miracles and have faith in God's timing.
- Do not audit life. Show up and make the most of it now.
- Growing old beats the alternative—dying young.
- Your children get only one childhood. Make it memorable.
- Get outside every day. Miracles are waiting everywhere.
- If we all threw our problems in a pile and saw everyone else's, we would grab ours back.
- Envy is a waste of time. You already have all you need.
- The best is yet to come.
- No matter how you feel, get up, dress up, and show up.
- Life isn't tied with a bow, but it's still a gift.

This book will take you through extraordinary experiences I encountered as a public safety professional. I did not think people would behave the way they did, but I learned that they could, they will, and they did.

CHAPTER 2
Emergency Services and the Community

"Life is change. Growth is optional. Choose wisely."
—Karen Kaiser Clark

Firefighting is a career that can make you feel proud and accomplished, a career for which people have a lot of respect. In order to be a firefighter, you must be in shape, prepared, experienced, and ready to deal with your job emotionally, mentally, and physically. After embarking on this career path, a number of individuals soon find out that firefighting may not be the best fit for them, because of routinely subjecting themselves to the risks of fire, smoke inhalation, collapsing buildings, the lack of interpersonal relationships, failing to follow orders, and just being an unethical person.

Today's fire service has decades of research behind it, making the process less dangerous than our fathers' and grandfathers' profession. Perhaps the foremost advantage of being a firefighter is the opportunity to save the lives of others on a regular basis, a satisfaction that imbues the job with meaning. Recognized for their bravery and their contribution to others, firefighters enjoy the esteem of their communities and of society. While this is an admirable position, some firefighters find themselves in a routine and take their frustrations out on fire department management and other leadership personnel. These firefighters feel that management placed them in an uncomfortable role, thus encouraging the firefighter to do what he must to turn the tables. These individuals are never satisfied and seek to destroy other people's hard work.

Although dangerous, firefighting is also exciting. Racing to the scene of a fire, bashing down a door with an ax, charging into a burning building—these are the playtime fantasies of boys (and some girls) everywhere. Few professions will pay employees to engage in such dangerous adventures. In the course of relying on each other, firefighters typically develop a deep sense of camaraderie and teamwork.

This fraternal sense extends both to one's immediate fire company and to the profession as a whole, with firefighters everywhere sharing a mutual respect for their brothers and sisters in red. This behavior also sometimes extends to lying, cheating, not being honest, and constructing scenarios which are designed to benefit the firefighting team and not the organization as a whole.

According to the Bureau of Labor Statistics, firefighting is a popular profession in part because individuals entering the field are not required to attain advanced levels of education. Many departments require individuals to hold only a high school diploma, rather than a full college degree. The results are some uneducated individuals with their own agenda, willing to take on any crusade, ethical or not.

Firefighters generally receive a good salary and excellent benefits. According to the Bureau of Labor Statistics, firefighters can earn upward of $100,000 per year and have excellent job security. The profession is in great demand, and approximately two-thirds of firefighters are members of unions, which help them fight against layoffs and gain extraordinary benefits—greater than others in the public and private sector.

Firefighters are often given very flexible schedules. Many career firefighters work only ten days a month, giving them significant time to take on other jobs. Because fires break out intermittently, many non-unionized volunteer firefighters will remain on-call for certain periods of time while performing little actual work. This down time permits firefighters to freely and creatively develop frauds on how they can benefit as a team.

According to the Fire Service Reputation Management white paper, "the nation's fire service has long been held in justifiably high esteem. This reputation has been hard earned. The fire service is that "rock of stability" to which the public knows to turn during the upheaval of a crisis—be that crisis a dwelling fire, rescue, natural disaster, or medical emergency. Fire service members unflinchingly charge into those situations from which others flee. We render these services to a grateful nation. The public, be it those who have been aided directly by the fire service or all the others who have merely borne witness to fire service heroics on the nightly news, is thankful that we are here and ready to serve at their beck and call. However, not all is well, for that hard-earned respect is easily lost."

It does not take much for those few firefighters who disregard the public service component of the fire service mission to undermine the hard-earned respect and support garnered by all the others that the fire service has strived to attain. Disturbing headlines increasingly report sensational stories of firefighters acting not selflessly and heroically, but rather selfishly and irresponsibly. The Fire Service Reputation Management white paper is intended as a wake-up call to the fire service. The detrimental impact from fire service members who engage in unethical, immoral, inappropriate, or criminal activities reflects back not just to these individuals but also to their departments and the fire service as a whole.

I entered the fire service in the mid-1970s. At that time, President Jimmy Carter was promoting his jobs incentive plan, the Comprehensive Education and Training Act (CETA) program. This program was designed to assist in creating jobs, and it permitted strapped jurisdictions to employ individuals for a period of three years—with the final year having the jurisdiction picking up the person in gainful employment. I was one of these individuals, and this is how I started my career.

The organization that employed me had a long tradition of fire service culture, with an emphasis on developing positive behavior by all individuals. While we as young recruits had a lot to learn, we soon learned the meaning of loyalty, friendship, courtesy, and being dependable, responsible, and accountable for our actions. Over the years, I found that these traits are no longer common in the fire service—in fact, just the opposite.

In the 1980s, public-sector collective bargaining was introduced to a number of states. We in the fire service found ourselves in a difficult situation. As a team, do we file for recognition with the International Association of Firefighters union or do we act as a stand-alone bargaining unit? In our organization, we decided to stand alone as an in-house bargaining unit, mainly because we felt proud to have a job, did not have conflicts with fire management, were generally pleased with our work, and appreciated the fact that we had elected and appointed senior officials willing to work with us.

During my career, I found that individual behaviors differ and the environment helps set their tone. I was disappointed in not only the firefighters' behaviors, but also those of the elected officials who, by law, had to have a fire department but were unwilling to invest in the organization. I found a number of elected officials to have large egos, and they did whatever it took to look good in the public eye. They would actually engage in unethical behaviors, just to have their hired legal team—at the taxpayers' expense—create a loophole for them to place blame. These people are known as being made of Teflon.

In my first twenty years of service, my wife and I raised a family, contributed to our community, and developed and maintained strong family values. I completed my bachelor's and master's degree and graduated from the National Fire Academy Executive Fire Officer Program. I recognized that if I want to improve myself, higher education was the correct path. As such, I gained a number of mentors throughout the country and look up to their wisdom and maturity still today.

I began as a firefighter/emergency medical technician, rose through the ranks, and left one department to work for another as an assistant fire chief, where I was introduced to the chief fire officer's role. Promotions in the fire service are sparse. Either you had to know someone or you had to work your tail off and compete against colleagues searching for the same thing. As an assistant fire chief, my then fire chief came to me with an opportunity that would change my life.

He stated that a community just north of us was looking for an ethical, moralistic, and knowledgeable individual to lead their fire department. I took his advice and the advice of my mentors and applied for this position. After an intense selection process, I rose to the top and was selected to lead this organization.

I viewed this community as one needing fire and emergency-service leadership, since the organization was growing exponentially, and they still were utilizing part-time and on-call volunteers. The times have definitely changed, and unfortunately, the community's leadership team had no clue on how to transform it.

The Packer Township Fire Protection District is a township-run organization covering the city of Throop, Pennsylvania. In Pennsylvania, the statutory law dictates that the township is responsible for providing emergency services (fire/EMS); a city *may* provide the service but is not required to do so.

The City of Throop and Packer Township are similar to most combined communities throughout America—it has a suburban/urban feel for most of the city, primarily a bedroom-community feel for the township, with some business and light industry sprinkled in designated pockets. Packer is mostly a rural township, bordering the city of Throop to the east.

In 1988, the Packer Township Fire Protection District (the private "Fire Company" as it was previously named) came under Packer Township Board of Trustee control, after financial issues arose. All of the existing members became public employees on January 1, 1988 and were unhappy that they had lost control.

Packer Township is governed by a three-member board of trustees, who are elected in November of odd-numbered years to a four-year term beginning on the following January 1. Two officials are elected in the year after the presidential election, and one is elected in the year before it. There is also an elected township fiscal officer who serves a four-year term beginning on April 1 of the year after the election, which is held in November of the year before the presidential election.

One of the first orders of business for the Packer Township Board of Trustees was to establish a fire chief to oversee the organization. The Richmond County law states:

Fire protection services, the board of trustees may establish all necessary rules to guard against the occurrence of fires and to protect the property and lives of the citizens against damage and accidents, and may, with the approval of the specifications by the prosecuting attorney, with the approval of the specifications by the Township's law director, purchase, lease, lease with an option to purchase, or otherwise provide any fire apparatus, mechanical resuscitators, or other equipment, appliances, materials, fire hydrants, and water supply for fire-fighting purposes that seems advisable to the board.

The board of trustees shall provide for the care and maintenance of fire equipment, and, for these purposes, may purchase, lease, lease with an option to purchase, or construct and maintain necessary buildings, and it may establish and maintain lines of fire-alarm communications within the limits of the Township. The board of trustees may employ one or more persons to maintain and operate fire-fighting equipment, or it may enter into an agreement with a volunteer fire company for the use and operation of fire-fighting equipment. The board of trustees may compensate the members of a volunteer fire company on any basis and in any amount that it considers equitable.

Under the previous private fire company, all of the employees were volunteers and earned an annual stipend. The fire chief was a retired local businessman. The board of trustees asked the fire chief to become full time, but he declined. Instead, the board of trustees hired a full-time assistant chief, who later became the fire chief and the source of misery.

The fire department was primarily a social organization, now being directed by the elected officials of the township. Packer Township (geographically) extends throughout the city of Throop and thus provided the fire/EMS services for both the city of Throop and all of Packer Township.

For decades, the Packer Township Fire Company, a private, independent fire department, contracted with Packer Township for service. As you might imagine, change is hard—especially for volunteers who have provided an invaluable service for so many years. This venture is economically in line with providing the best services with the resources available to the public; however, the Packer Township board of trustees did not calculate the interpersonal reaction of these safety personnel when they passed this legislation.

The day-to-day Packer Township government operations were led by Peter Graywater, the township administrator, who works at the sole discretion of the Packer Township board of trustees. Graywater, having a bachelor of arts degree, has been the town administrator for Packer Township for over fifteen years and is not affiliated with any credentialing organizations like the International City/Township Managers Association.

Packer Township Fire Protection District's first fire chief was a volunteer firefighter, backed up by a full-time assistant chief. Frank Lynn, the Packer Township assistant township administrator and safety director, told me of a number of occasions when the assistant fire chief would be in conflict with the fire chief, which developed into a stressed environment. As time progressed, the volunteer fire chief retired, and the assistant chief, after a selection process, was hired as the new fire chief. This selection process apparently had its own issues.

Frank Lynn is the assistant township administrator and safety director. Lynn graduated from Oklahoma State University with a bachelor's degree in criminology and was initially hired as a Packer Township police officer. Lynn found himself in the first of many conflicts with Peter Graywater over the amount of vacation time that the township is required to accept from Lynn's previous employment with the Orange Township Police Department.

This issue escalated to the point that Lynn and the Fraternal Order of Police union filed a claim in the Richmond County Common Pleas Court. Lynn won, and this was a turning point. Peter Graywater then asked Lynn to join his team and become the assistant township administrator. Frank Lynn's position included working on legal and human-resource issues for Packer Township.

As the position of fire chief was presented, Peter Graywater told the then assistant fire chief, Thomas Vandyke, that if he wanted the position, he would have to partake in the selection process. This apparently did not sit well with Thomas Vandyke, who felt he was the only person appropriate for the fire chief position. When he did not get his way, he withdrew his application.

Thomas Vandyke lived within the city of Throop and was a firefighter for Packer Township. Vandyke had ultimately gained the assistant fire chief position for the Packer Township Fire Company and was seeking to improve the department's capabilities. During the initial fire chief application process, board of trustee's president Clark Neil called Thomas Vandyke into his office, and before you know it, he had hired him as the fire chief.

As time passed, under Vandyke's leadership, morale suffered, and the equipment was not kept in a state of operational readiness. According to Lynn and Graywater, Vandyke had first started with inappropriate behavior by purchasing three leather helmets, one white helmet (for himself), and two red helmets, (one for Captains Brandon Clinton and Michael Baum). These helmets cost $500 each.

It was later discovered that Vandyke had purchased these expensive helmets without authorization. When Peter Graywater found out about this unauthorized purchase, not only did he become livid, but he also ordered these helmets be returned to the vendor and the taxpayers' money be returned.

According to Brandon Clinton, one of Vandyke's fire captains, this did not occur; the leather helmets were at Vandyke, Clinton, and Baum's homes. Peter Graywater ordered Clinton to go to Vandyke's house and get these helmets, or Peter Graywater would file theft charges against Vandyke. This was the beginning of the tail-wagging-the-dog issues, which plagued and progressed for years to come. I had no previous knowledge of any of Vandyke's antics and was quite surprised a fire chief would act with such disregard to the taxpayer's hard-earned money.

Soon after taking office in January 1997, I called the former fire chief, to provide me with some insight during his tenure. Initially, Vandyke had agreed to meet with me, but on the day he was to arrive, he called me, telling me that he was not going to show up and that he was going to do everything in his power to get me fired.

Vandyke even went on to say that I "would no longer be fire chief before year's end." I found this behavior quite disturbing, and I contemplated his motivation. During my research, I discovered the following documents, which in my opinion, speak about Vandyke's behavior and his irrational train of thought.

> *William MacNeil*
> *Trevor Fire Protection District*

> *Dear Willy,*

> *As you are well aware, I have accepted the position of firefighter/ paramedic with a neighboring fire department. This decision was made with your assistance, which I cannot thank you enough. Both my wife and I cannot express our gratitude for the time you took to listen to my ranting and ravings about the Packer Township Administrators and elected officials. Your patience and insight, as well as your ability to sift through the many negative situations I had to endure, is most appreciated.*

> *Without a doubt, one of the hardest aspects of leaving my fire chiefs job is after having endured over eight years within the county, we are finally beginning to get the other fire chiefs in this county, to stop treating our profession as a good old boy social club.*

> *Thank you again for your time and I ask that you do me a favor—please keep an eye on **MY** department, whom ever takes my place. **Please make sure that this person does not screw things up.** Thanks again for your help.*

> *Thomas Vandyke, Fire Chief*
> *Packer Township Fire Protection District*

It appears that even though Vandyke was willing to move on, he still felt that the Packer Township Fire Protection Organization was *his and his alone.* This narrow-minded approach is characteristic of a person who believes that he is the single reason why the organization works.

"Narcissism" is a term with a wide range of meanings, depending on whether it is used to describe a central concept of psychoanalytic theory, a mental condition, a social or cultural problem, or simply a personality trait. Except in the sense of primary narcissism or healthy self-love, narcissism is usually used to describe some kind of problem in a person's relationships with self and others. In everyday speech, narcissism often means inflated self-importance, egotism, vanity, conceit, or simple selfishness.

Vandyke had a number of issues with individuals. He filed a complaint against Michael Baum, his third-in-command captain, for not following orders. As the inquiry proceeded, it was discovered that Thomas Vandyke had falsely accused Baum, and the issue was dismissed.

Brandon Clinton was Vandyke's second-in-command captain, mainly responsible for emergency medical service, equipment, and documentation. Baum earned a bachelor's degree in education and was a teacher at the Austin High School before coming to Packer Township.

According to the Fire Service Reputation Management white paper, poor personal decision-making by individuals that leads to public embarrassment (or worse) might not, at first, appear to be a threat to the welfare or reputation of the fire service. If a firefighter is arrested for selling drugs from a fire station in a distant state, is that really a problem? If a group of firefighters uses an emergency medical service backboard device as a board to slide down a flight of steps at the firehouse, is this really a problem? It may not have been in the past, but now, when news proliferates quickly via many delivery methods, it can and often does have state and possibly national repercussions.

Moreover, even incidents that occur off duty and outside the scope of the fire service involving members of the profession bring similar disrepute. Stories that in the recent past the media would not have even covered at all now yield banner headlines that shout, "Firefighter cited for operating a motor vehicle while under the influence." This can now bring embarrassment to a fire department.

In further researching Vandyke, I was provided a document by fellow fire chief and township administrator Mike Carney. When Carney was the president of the Richmond County Fire Chiefs Association, he apparently had issues with Vandyke as well. Here are his written comments:

> *Chief Ralph Randy, President*
> *Richmond County Fire Chiefs Association*
>
> *Dear Ralph,*
>
> *I am in receipt of your letter dated February 24, which was evidently written on behalf of the 6 fire chiefs who attended at the last county chiefs meeting. As you read my response to the 'groups' concerns, please keep in mind that my responses are directed not at you personally but rather the chief's association as an organization.*
>
> *Your letter references the 'great deal of activity that requires input from all members'. While I agree 100% with this statement, you left out one vital addition to the sentence replace 'input' with 'agreement'. Never in my life have I experienced a group of individuals who can consistently fail to agree on literally every aspect of any project or problem as the Richmond County Fire Chief's.*
>
> *When I was originally hired, I attend my first Richmond County Fire Chief's meeting. Filled with hopes and expectations, I listened to a room of me who I did not know; speak of timely issues such as the lack of hazardous materials response capability, and of the complaints of a lack of quality communications system, and protocol. I must say that I was extremely impressed with this group's determination to move forward and address these important issues.*
>
> *Over five years later, at my last chief's meeting I listened to a room of men who I do know speak of timely issues such as the lack of a hazardous materials response capability, and of the complaints of a lack of a quality communication system, and protocol. Gee, sound familiar?*
>
> *Your letter hints at the need for the attendance to be better so that the group may speak in a stronger, more unified voice. While this would be a nice objective, you know as well as that, nothing of the sort will ever happen. As part of preparing this letter, I went back over the past 5 years and reviewed the minutes for the meeting. As I reviewed these documents, I was once again*

reminded of why I elect to use my evening hour in the pursuit of more productive efforts, as opposed to listening to a group of people discuss (?) the same issues over and over again.

At the risk of sounding too sarcastic, allow me to illustrate to you some of my thoughts on this organization. In addition to the immense progress realized as a direct result of the intensive efforts of our group in communications and hazardous material response, there are other areas, which are very clear indicators of our ability to work together and agree.

1. *In response to the agreed upon deed to reconfigure and redesign the means by which we identify radio numbers of the county radio system, a select committee worked for months and months on designing what was felt to be a better way. Shortly after everyone on the county system agreed that as usual "something should be done," the very same people began arguing about the efforts and results.*

   Eventually, after much work, heartburn, and Rolaids, the premier radio identifier system was presented. Not only was it almost identical to the existing system, but the group still complained!

   The very organization that stated the extreme need to redesign the radio identifying system was now complaining about the end-result, more amusingly, they were complaining about the end result which they themselves brought about. This town doesn't like being called this name. That person doesn't like being this number where do you guys get off?

   Most assuredly, common terminology has been realized, but as I listen to county primary, everyone isn't doing it the same even now. I also have a $5.00 bet that it will be even worse in 6 months when someone doesn't like the way someone says that, so we'll just change it. Laugh if you want, but I have seen it happen too many times in the past.

2. *Work and accomplishments that have been realized are typically accomplished by the efforts of other people or organizations. Most often, the chief's group is a trailing end to the work being done by others, as opposed to a leader. Even worse, these outside organizations are often times*

scorned for tackling and addressing these issues by the very people who benefit the most from their work, namely the Richmond County Fire Chiefs. The Richmond County Chief's consistently bang the drum, that the outside organization do not cooperate with the chief's, or conduct themselves in a manner which is deemed 'in our best interest. Well gentlemen, does the phrase "look at the kettle called the pot black" mean anything to you?

3. *The main effort of the organization, as it consistently emphasized at meetings is to discredit, and criticize people and organizations outside your own. How many examples of this do you need? With the receipt of this particular letter, I would know appear that while your group has successfully alienated themselves from all of their support groups outside of the organization, you are now turning your attention toward the members of the organization itself. If you keep this trend up, you are not going to have a group. Then whom will you complain about—yourself?*

4. *Another interesting little observation I conducted, which a few other Chief's know about as well, I timed the duration of the last couple of meetings I have attended. Without exception, the meetings lasted less than 35 minutes, and sure, this included the meal! Now really, how much important work and projects can a group discuss in 35 minutes?*

5. *Finally, this group consistently is quite content with sticking their head in the sand when it comes to dealing with issues they do not understand, or when they are being faced with a mandated requirement that they chose to ignore. This is known as 'ostrich management', and has been perfected right here in the Richmond County Chief's Association. Ultimately, we argue and complain about the lack of effort, work, and commitment of other outside people and organizations, while in face we are the absolute worst offenders of this complaint.*

Do not even attempt to bring the age-old argument of "well if more Chief's would attend the meetings, we could realize better progress." You know as well as I that this argument holds absolutely no truth whatsoever. There have been several meetings where the chiefs have all left the meeting after much discussion and argument with only two agreements:

1. *Something must be done on someone's part, but not ours because it's not our fault, and,*
2. *Who is serving dinner next month?*

   Due to this organizations lack of ability at even agreeing with ourselves, we have quite sufficiently been able to paint a picture throughout the County as a useless organization. The local elected officials know it, the county elected officials know it, local, and county appointed officials know it, and now I truly believe that many of the chief's themselves know it. Why else is your attendance in the state that it is? Quite simply, they are sick of it, they have better means by which to achieve their needs, and the meetings are simply a waste of time.

   With reference to the members concerns regarding our volunteer fire company's status with Richmond County Firefighters Association, I would strongly suggest that the Richmond County Firefighters Association fight their own battle with the members of the Volunteer Fire Company. I have no input into this organization, nor do I wish to get involved in yet another organization such as that. The decision to exit the Firefighters Association was that of the group of personnel who belong to the company, for your information, the Volunteer Fire District has never recognized the county organization. It is viewed as a social group.

   In closing, as for my department's status with the chief's organization, it is active. Had any member of this fine group thought to ask in a more polite and direct methods, you would have found that you are meeting night's conflict with my requirement to be in attendance at my Board of Trustee meetings, which are held on the same night. As for having another member attend in my absence, in the past none of my personnel has made me mad enough to punish them in this cruel way. I will assure you that as available, I will attend these meetings. I do in fact look forward to receiving the minutes of the meetings, which I cannot attend, as is provided to me via the by-laws of the organization. When there is significant issue on the table which requires a consensus of all chief's, I will assure you that I will make every effort to attend and help the cause of the organization. Until that time however, I will get my meals at home.

Prepared as per Your Request,
Thomas Vandyke, Fire Chief
Packer Township Fire Protection District

Based on Vandyke's letters, one could categorize his behavior as trying to be a martyr. It appears that he felt so betrayed that he had to fall on the sword—take one for the team, engage himself in overwhelming suffering, rather than follow directions. He even looked for sympathy in every avenue he could.

Lynn showed me a newspaper article, illustrating the way he had been mistreated by the Packer Township board of trustees and others. Vandyke even had a picture of himself holding a helmet that Vandyke stated "was given to [him] by his loyal firefighters as an outward sign of support."

As you might imagine, the stage for any person to come into this organization and lead it to prosperity was going to be a challenge.

CHAPTER 3
Not Everyone's Happy

"Whenever one finds oneself inclined to bitterness,
it is a sign of emotional failure."
—*Bertrand Russell*

As a newly promoted fire chief, I recognized that I needed to accept individual behaviors (good and bad) of people, and to mold them into a considerate, conscious, and morally engaged organization. To help facilitate this, I met with the employees of the Fire Protection District to help formulate a positive plan for change.

I took the time (day, night, and weekends) to meet with every member of our organization (except for Brandon Clinton, second in command, who said he did not want to meet with me), and asked them what they believed were the top three items or issues most important to them. The results are:

Needed equipment (ladder/EMS unit):	25%
Training (fire and EMS):	27%
Additional station:	1%
Pay raises	8%
Leadership/discipline:	42%
Staffing (all shifts):	50%

I was surprised that the members did not want more money—they wanted the opportunity to be part of a thriving, well-trained, and educated organization for which they can be proud to work.

To lead in facilitating a new direction, in April 1997, the Packer

Township Fire Protection District, under my leadership, embarked on a strategic planning process. It was designed to help better define our capabilities and to develop recommendations to move our organization forward. To do this, we assembled the department supervisors for a leadership retreat, designed to help identify our roles as emergency service providers and to collaborate and have collective input on the future direction of our organization.

The leadership team comprised officers and supervisors serving as leaders, mentors, and coaches for the entire organization.

In the beginning, all of the fire officers and supervisors decided to maximize our resources and services we provide through goals, objectives, and programs. The leadership team spent an entire weekend brainstorming, researching, and building consensus on the future direction of the Fire Protection District. We all felt that we were embarking on a new vision for providing services to the citizens and visitors who depend on us.

Our established motto was "Color outside the lines through empowerment." We know that many times, citizens feel that all they hear from government is what they *can't do*—so we made it our mission to become an agency people can depend on and provide a "can-do" service.

At the end of the process, we asked individuals to review the plan carefully. We hoped that they would take this information and share their views and ideas. The entire Packer Township Fire Protection District leadership team signed this document.

It was interesting to see the officers and supervisors all signing the strategic plan. I used this experience and wrote my fourth-year applied-research project for the National Fire Academy Executive Fire Officer Program in Emmitsburg, Maryland, on this venture. I had no idea that there were thieves among the ranks of the Packer Township Fire Protection District.

I soon discovered to my surprise that some of our personnel actually broke into my office and stole a copy of my applied research project to help escalate their cause. This act confirmed to me that these people would do anything to get their way and to elevate their cause.

The leadership retreat did yield some organizational benefits, such as creating and refining our new organizational mission statement. The mission statement of any organization is essential to ensure that the general theme and principles for which an organization stands are descriptive of their purpose. Once the ideas for the future, most critical issues for the Fire Protection District, strengths of the Fire Protection District, critical customer needs, important functions/services, and most importantly tools/means of meeting customer needs were identified, it was time to institute a mission statement.

We agreed that the mission statement must convey a) Leadership relays information members need to know about the organization, and b) Leadership relays information to the public about the organization.

After lengthy discussion, and through a consensus process, the Packer Township Fire Protection District mission statement was developed to read:

> *"The mission of the Packer Township Fire Protection District is to provide the highest level of emergency services, in an efficient and cost effective manner, utilizing the resources provided by the Community."*

The Packer Township Fire Protection District strategic planning process was a new approach for the department that began to define and develop programs that will lead the organization into its future. From this, the first Packer Township Fire Protection District leadership team retreat became involved in short- and long-range planning sessions, looking into operational management problems, management objectives, benchmarking, officer responsibilities, staff development, brainstorming, and ways to initiate the "Packer Fire Protection District Involvement" process. Over these two days, we discussed:

- team-building, assessment review, and sensitive issues
- strategic planning, mission and job descriptions
- the "Packer Involvement" process
- working as a team
- *7 Habits of Highly Effective Leaders*
- assessment review (interview surveys)
- employee assistance program: the supervisor's role
- sensitive issues: ethics, sexual harassment, cultural diversity, delegations
- performance reviews—service quality—benchmarking
- strategic planning—mission statement
- job descriptions and the "Packer Fire Protection District Involvement" process

As with any project, planning became the most important function of the strategic plan. Planning is a basic step in fire and EMS protection management. Timely and dynamic fire and EMS planning provides the basics for systematic control of current and future risks.

An effective township protection plan cannot be developed without input from each member of its organization. All organizations that have a major impact on the protection system should be involved, so their appropriate roles can be established and mutually agreed upon.

The tangible result of this planning process is a document, often called the strategic plan. An even more important outcome of this effort should be a dynamic, long-term planning process that can adjust to township demographics, land-development patterns, and technological changes.

The ability to project or predict future conditions that will affect the Fire Protection District is quite limited. Communities are dynamic. Change will influence the protection plan; therefore, the plan must be periodically reviewed, revised, and updated through an ongoing process that is well coordinated. "What do we have to do today to be ready for an uncertain tomorrow?" With this in mind, the Packer Township Fire Protection District identified the following four-step process for implementation of the strategic plan:

- Develop an annual budget that provides infrastructure review.
- Identify items that need immediate attention (short term).
- Identify methods in which to implement strategic plan.
- Review, revise, modify plan as necessary.

THE MOST CRITICAL CUSTOMER-ORIENTED NEEDS

As part of a customer-centered strategic planning process, it is imperative that critical customer needs are identified and compared to critical issues, strengths of the department, services, and programs being offered to our citizens. This is a key area to provide a true litmus test as to whether a department is providing what its customers need. Through a consensus process, the most critical customer needs identified by the leadership team are as follows:

- Life safety enhancement

- Education (citizens' action committees to inform others)
- Emergency intervention and mitigation
- Planning for and providing protection of the quality of life of our citizens

THE MOST IMPORTANT TOOLS AND MEANS OF MEETING CUSTOMER NEED

Through a consensus process, the following eight items were listed as the most important tools and means of meeting customer needs:

- Attitude (teamwork)
- Training and education of our personnel
- Facilities and equipment
- Personnel (quantity and quality)
- Planning (pro-action vs. reaction)
- Communications (internal and external)
- Life safety codes
- Public education/township services

PACKER FIRE PROTECTION DISTRICT INVOLVEMENT

Too many times, we hear that "management does not listen to my ideas and makes me feel unimportant." The Packer Township Fire Protection District, through our involvement process, eliminates the "Big Brother" image by empowering personnel in specific areas.

The "Packer Fire Protection District Involvement" process is primarily broken down into two areas: Emergency and Support Services Division and Management and Information Services Division. Each division has eight to nine areas of specialization. Each specialist is responsible for the implementation and ongoing maintenance of each project, thus promoting empowerment.

GOALS AND OBJECTIVES

In order to accomplish the Packer Township Fire Protection District mission, it is imperative to have specific goals and objectives, which provide adequate direction to the staff and to the leadership team relative to what needs to be accomplished in the future. The leadership team, through a consensus process, established the following goals and objectives:

Goal 1: Enhance the quality of life to the internal and external customers

- Re-evaluate existing response policies (effectiveness)
- Initiate "duty officer" program, 24 hours a day, 7 days a week
- Re-evaluate scheduling of existing "in house" crews
- Develop a recruitment program
- Re-evaluate compensation for employees (market analysis)

Goal 2: Increase the flow of information to and from the department
- Conduct weekly executive leadership team meetings
- Conduct monthly leadership team meetings (all officers)
- Conduct semi-annual "State of the Department" address (all members)
- Publish the department newsletter (monthly or bimonthly)
- Submit articles/press releases to local newspaper
- Develop a media plan using public service announcements (PSAs)
- Video/slide series of Fire Protection District actions/ involvements

Goal 3: Develop a system that increases fiscal inflows and resource accountability to the Fire Protection District
- Research alternative means of Fire Protection District funding
- Submit applications to "traditional" annual grants
- Revisit the budget quarterly for cost effectiveness and/or benefits to the district

Goal 4: Develop a user-friendly initial and in-service training program

- Redefine qualifications for firefighter, emergency medical technician, and paramedic
- Redefine training requirements (scheduling, percentage per year) both fire/EMS
- Develop an "equivalency" program for outside fire/EMS training
- Develop specialized training programs (driver training, fire apparatus operation, standing orders)
- Instill the highest quality education and training

IN SUMMARY

The Packer Township Fire Protection District was embarking on a new adventure, one that would provide dividends to the internal and external customer of the city of Throop and Packer Township. In short, fire service organizations, much like a football team, are dependent upon the players doing their job.

Each person must be mentally and physically prepared for the tasks required of him. Practice and emphasis on the basics, enforcing the rules, seeking out natural leaders, delegating certain authority and responsibility, defining behavior that works, and rewarding it are key essentials for organizational advancement. This is exactly what the leadership team and members of the Packer Township Fire Protection District were striving for, whatever it takes—or so I was led to believe.

Unfortunately, however, some members of the leadership team clearly did not buy in to this strategic plan, incited some of our personnel to rear up, and cause havoc. Members of the old Packer Township Fire Company (and now members of the board of trustees-ruled Packer Township Fire Protection District) requested an organizational meeting with the Packer Township board of trustees, managers, and the media. Their goal was to have the elected officials listen to their complaints and to grandstand them to the media.

Certain individuals felt that the Fire Protection District leaders were taking away their way of life; in actuality, this was the furthest thing from the truth. They stereotyped me as the "wolf in sheep's clothing." Firefighters Sam Grubbs, Kellogg Anders, Pyle and Howard Goddard, Jennifer Leach, and Brandon Clinton (who was a career captain of the

Fire Protection District and second in command), were advocating that I, the fire chief, was taking the Fire Protection District in the wrong direction, and they did not want to be part of this. In fact, they accused me of being insensitive to their needs.

These individuals did not want the organization to move forward and to be accountable for their actions. They wanted the trustees to let them run the organization as they saw fit, with little supervision. This is one of the reasons why there was a need to hire a person from outside of the organization to correct this negative behavior, and the firefighters did not appreciate this.

I found it interesting that at one moment, we had officers and supervisors wanting to move the organization in an orderly, forward fashion, yet they were telling the cadre that the direction we were taking is wrong for them and the Township. This reminded me of the song "Smiling Faces" from the Temptations.

I went back to the survey instruments I used to help determine what traits our officers possess, to help understand why there were two-faced individuals within the organization. Gordon's Personality Inventory—GPI—measures personal qualities and values. Those tested answer questions on both descriptions of personal characteristics and what they think is important in life. Everyone has certain fundamental personality traits that can be measured, that are presumed stable over time and can be indicators how people will act at work.

Low scores are poor, while high scores are preferred. High and lower scores on each of the scales are interpreted as reflecting the following tendencies:

ASCENDANCY: High scores characterize individuals who are verbally ascendant, who adopt an active role in the group, who tend to make independent decisions and who are self-assured in relationships with others. Those who play a passive role in the group, who listen rather than talk, who lack self-confidence, who let others take the lead, and who tend to be overly dependent on other for advice, normally makes low scores.

RESPONSIBILITY: Individuals who are able to stick to the job assigned them, who are persevering and determined and who can be relied on, generally score high on this scale. Individuals who are unable to stick to tasks that do not interest them and who tend to be flighty or irresponsible typically make low scores.

EMOTIONAL STABILITY: High scores on this scale are generally made by individuals who are emotionally stable and relatively free from worries, anxieties, hypersensitivity, nervousness, and a low frustration tolerance. A very low score generally reflects poor emotional adjustment.

CAUTIOUSNESS: Individuals who are highly cautious, who consider matters very carefully before making decisions, and who do not like to take chances or run risks typically make high scores on this scale. Those who are impulsive, who act on the spontaneous, who make hurried or snap decisions, which enjoy taking chances, and who seek excitement normally score low on this scale.

ORIGINAL THINKING: High-scoring individuals generally like to work on difficult problems, are intellectually curious, enjoy thought-provoking questions and discussions, and like to think about new ideas. Those who score low dislike working on difficult or complicated problems and do not care particularly about acquiring knowledge and are not interested in thought-provoking questions or discussions.

PERSONAL RELATIONS: High scores typify those individuals who have faith and trust in people and who are tolerant, patient, and understanding. Low scores reflect a lack of trust or confidence in people and a tendency to be critical of others and to become annoyed or irritated by what others do.

Listed are the results of the personality and values qualifier.

	Daugherty	Clinton	Baum	Pickings
Ascendancy	78 %	18 %	13 %	25 %
Responsibility	97 %	13 %	27 %	20 %
Emotional Stability	97 %	13 %	31 %	19 %
Cautiousness	89 %	37 %	28 %	11 %
Original Thinking	84 %	22 %	16 %	32 %
Personal Relations	89 %	35 %	24 %	18 %

In my opinion, these scores reflect that a number of the Fire Protection District officers/supervisors are not as qualified as they thought they were.

It would appear that the low/poor-scoring traits are a reflection of poor leadership. Vandyke's right-hand man, Brandon Clinton, would often bring a tape recorder to meetings or conversations I attended. In fact, after our leadership retreat, Clinton felt so compelled that the organization was going in the wrong direction, he posted this comment:

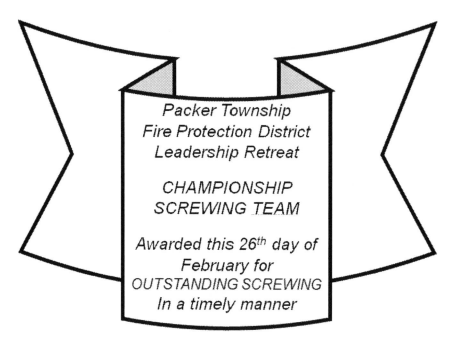

Packer Township
Fire Protection District
Leadership Retreat

CHAMPIONSHIP
SCREWING TEAM

Awarded this 26th day of
February for
OUTSTANDING SCREWING
In a timely manner

From when I first began this journey, I made it a point not to forget where my roots were and to bring a positive change to not only the citizens, but to the fire department cadre. I began to realize that there are some deep-seeded interpersonal issues with a number of the members, and with the Management as a whole.

No one was willing to talk to one another—Management loved talking **AT** their employees, and in my opinion, enjoyed flexing their muscles. This environment is not healthy for what should be an equitable atmosphere.

Over my tenure as Fire Chief, I witnessed over eight Police Chiefs (acting or actual) come and go through Packer Township. Lynn, the Assistant Township Administrator and Safety Director, told me that one of the Police Chiefs was found to have sexual relations with a Throop Police Dispatcher at her place of employment one evening.

In another situation, Police Chief Ian York informed me that he was told by the Packer Township Board of Trustees, to fire his second in command, Lieutenant Marcus Martin, since Marcus would not deviate from the law. Marcus Martin was required to discipline some of the police officer for what the Board of Trustees indicated as an infraction but would not be specific.

Chief York stated that he backed Lieutenant Martin, so the Board of Trustees fired Police Chief York instead. Subsequently, Lynn was then appointed acting Police Chief in many of these occasions. Chief York later told me this information and told me to watch my back—you cannot trust Peter Graywater or Frank Lynn.

The Packer Township Administrator Peter Graywater has a tendency to spin whatever topic is at hand. I once tried to get Peter Graywater and Frank Lynn to recognize the importance of having an on-going supervisory leadership and "higher education" training opportunities, just to have Lynn and Graywater take this request to the Board of Trustees, with the result being "NO."

They said that they had to pay for their education (except for Arthur Bode that only finished high school), so the firefighters can pay for their own higher education. Furthermore, do not ever bring this issue up again.

I noticed early on that there is a power struggle between Peter Graywater and Frank Lynn. Lynn obtained his job after taking Peter Graywater to court over vacation time accrual—Lynn won. To further illustrate the towering ego of Peter Graywater—he would tell of the department heads that Clark Neil was the "Chairman of the Board" (like Frank Sinatra)—but he (Peter Graywater) is to be address as the "President of Packer Township." It is sad on how shallow Peter Graywater had become.

The Packer Township management definitely had their favorites. During a time of hiring a career full-time firefighter replacement, I had Frank Lynn tell me to recommend hiring one of our part-time firefighters. This firefighter, Aaron Watt, failed the written examination and was (legally and ethically) dismissed from further consideration. Frank Lynn stated that Aaron is a friend of Trustee Arthur Bode, and if I wanted to keep my job, I needed to recommend Aaron to get the firefighter job. While I tried to stay true to my ethical beliefs, the Packer Township Trustees hired Aaron in lieu of a more qualified candidate.

On one occasion, an unknown person was making inappropriate statements about me on the VHF radio system, and Frank Lynn stated that the Township would conduct an investigation. Six months later, Frank Lynn said that, "There is nothing they can do" but failed to investigate the incident.

Firefighter Sam Grubbs, one of the Fire Protection District's full-time employees, was getting married over a Memorial Day weekend, and he wanted Aaron Watt to attend his special event. To help celebrate this occasion, my wife and I purchased a $100 crystal picture frame and a congratulations card for Sam and his wife.

Aaron Watt was unable to secure a replacement firefighter for his shift and was unable to make this special event.

Because of the frustrated firefighters, Sam Grubbs returned my family's gift with a note stating, "Thanks for the thought, Chief, but a better gift would have been to let Aaron Watt attend the reception with his wife.

"You can keep the gift and give it to someone who might believe you are sincere.

Sincerely, Sam Grubbs."

The Packer Township administrators and elected officials would send the Packer Township employees, via US Mail, a Christmas card and a card on their birthday. Every year, without fail, part-time firefighter Pyle Goddard would receive his cards and place them in my department mailbox. Pyle Goddard would place a note on the cards saying that he did not like any of us and asking to stop sending the cards. I took the card, every time, back to Frank Lynn; he would make some explanative and then place the cards in Pyle Goddard's personnel file.

While completing my fourth-year executive fire officer applied-research project for the National Fire Academy, I decided to discuss the cultures of a combination fire department. My project, "Protecting with Combination Services: A Study in Changing Cultures," was a snapshot of what I had experienced as fire chief in just two years.

When I completed and sent my project to the National Fire Academy, I soon discovered that some Packer Township firefighters broke into my office, took a copy of my project, and tried to elevate their cause by using my homework assignment against me and the direction I was moving the department.

Here is a copy of the letter Wayne Kirby sent back to us regarding one of "Packer Township's finest" behavior. This affirmed to me that these so-called "protectors of the township" were deviant, deceitful, only out for themselves, criminal-minded, and had lost their moral compass.

Mr. Peter Graywater, Administrator
Packer Township

On February 24, 1997, the United States Fire Administration's National Fire Academy, Executive Fire officer Program, received a telephone call from Packard Township Fire Protection District Firefighter Kellogg Anders, requesting information regarding an applied research project by Chief Kelly Daugherty. Specifically, he requested if we had in fact received Chief Kelly Daugherty applied research project and on what date. A staff member stated to him that this information could not be provided, and that he needed to speak directly to Chief Kelly Daugherty.

The staff member recorded Firefighter Kellogg Anders telephone number and stated that it would be necessary to contact me if he wanted to pursuit the matter. In fact, the staff person called me at home, as there was a sense of something awry regarding the nature and form of this inquiry.

When I returned to work the next day, I called Firefighter Kellogg Anders at the telephone number provided; there was no answer, and I left a telephone message. I have yet to receive a return call from Firefighter Kellogg Anders.

Sincerely,

Wayne Kirby
United States Fire Administration
National Fire Academy

In the mid-1990s, the International Association of Fire Chiefs posted a document titled "Fire Chief under Attack." This document highlighted the negative and truculent behavior of the International Association of Fire Fighters, their state organizations, and the women and men who proclaim to be "brothers." As such, Chief Richard Moreno of Tucson, Arizona, chairman of the IAFC Metropolitan Fire Chief's Association (1990–1991) states "the International Association of Fire Fighters promotes the undermining of fire chiefs by encouraging and lauding votes of no-confidence, political pressure, negative media campaigns, and the discrediting of Managements."

The IAFC further explains that the attempt to undermine the fire chief's personal and professional credibility within the political process and through the news media is often used in an effort to "soften up" management prior to contract negotiations. Often this tactic is used to resist the chief's efforts to implement changes in the department or as an attempt to oust the fire chief in favor of a candidate supported by the union. The issues behind the conflict are generally contrived or unusual situational factors, chosen specifically because the instigator knows that the "problem" is beyond the control of the fire chief.

The basic approach is to discredit, defame, demoralize, and isolate the fire chief, making management more difficult and casting doubt on the fire chief's credibility. The direct target audience is the elected political body. The public at large is the secondary audience to which the union will present itself as the only organization truly concerned with public safety. Union actions such as votes of no confidence and motions of censure amount to no more than a public trial without a jury or even a chance to answer the charges appropriately.

It is important to note that in most cases, chiefs who observe the status quo almost never come into conflict, while the chief who tries to change the system for the better is attacked viciously and repeatedly. These attacks can be particularly destructive. The progressive chief is likely to be highly dedicated to the mission and makes a strong personal commitment to solving problems and improving conditions. In addition to the direct impacts, the personal attacks and hostile atmosphere often demoralize the individual chief and can result in understandable problems with self-esteem and personal relationships. These problems may extend to the chief's family members, close friends, and supporters within the department.

If the union tactics are successful in causing the chief's dismissal or resignation, the IAFF may even go further, inhibiting the individual's attempts to find a new job. This has been done through publicizing the conflict in areas where the chief seeks employment, or by submitting motions of censure against the chief during the IAFF annual convention. Many appointing authorities are reluctant to select a fire chief who has a poor record of accomplishment in labor relations, particularly if the local union voices strong objections toward that individual.

In one case, the attacking local provided a dossier to a chief-selection board that contained damaging, one-sided material on the chief. While these actions could be judged a violation of the candidate's civil rights, it is extremely difficult to prove that a candidate was not accepted because of deliberate harassment by a union. It is evident that the IAFF and some of its locals have little concern for ethical considerations of the tactics employed to achieve their objectives. Issues are contrived or severely misrepresented, attacking the fire chief simply to obstruct his ability to manage the fire department.

In the traditional paramilitary organization of the fire department, many of these tactics would have been judged as insubordination and would have resulted in severe disciplinary actions. However, in present reality, there are few limits on the behavior of an employee organization or its leadership. Conversely, as a public official, the fire chief is always subject to close scrutiny and must exercise caution in imposing disciplinary actions.

It appears that IAFF will support its locals at the national level and will employ any tactics necessary to support their objectives without regard to ethics or to the personal consequences to the targeted individual. While the IAFF openly professes an "enlightened" approach to labor-management relations, it has been actively involved in several disputes where the issues were contrary to the organization's espoused positions and the tactics involved deliberately misrepresented the facts. National leaders of the IAFF have allowed their names to be used with personal quotations attached to press releases directed against individual chiefs. The official statement usually suggests that a "problem" has been investigated by the IAFF, although in most cases, the fire chief is never contacted by anyone from the IAFF, much less someone claiming to be an investigator.

The fire chief is legally bound by ethical considerations. If a fire chief is found to have violated the civil rights of employees, to fabricate stories about their conduct or performance, or to misrepresent situations to damage the reputations of union officers, the chief can and should be held liable. That accountability is to the jurisdiction and to the political body as well as to public opinion. Accountability is an important aspect of the fire chief's work environment, including off-duty personal behavior.

The sad part of this issue is that the Packer Township management has failed to do their job and continues to artificially investigate matters of great importance. Peter Graywater feels that throwing paper at the situation will solve their problems—well, it has not. The following is the paper parade, which led to more internal hostility. Thomas Vandyke's legacy was plagued with controversy. According to the Packer Township Fire Protection District officers, Vandyke drove his staff vehicle through an interstate highway median one day and destroyed the undercarriage. Vandyke is known for leaving fire apparatus in disrepair—leaving one engine without an air filter. The apparatus repairperson told me that Vandyke would often state, "If the engine is out of service for any length of time, then the board of trustees will let me buy what I want."

Vandyke never even made sure that the apparatus was officially licensed or deeded to the township; this was one of my first orders of business as the new fire chief. Vandyke has demoralized individuals in the presence of others and disobeyed direct orders by allowing his family to travel in his staff vehicle. It is a direct violation and liability for non-township employees to ride in township-owned vehicles. However, Vandyke had engaged in this type of behavior on a number of documented occasions. Thomas Vandyke's role was to be a coach, mentor, and leader; however, he left the organization crippled, splintered, and disabled.

Thomas Vandyke was a friend of the one-time mayor of the city of Throop, Brandon Shell. Mayor Shell took me to dinner one night, asking me the focus of our organization. He stated it was his goal to split the Fire Protection District from the township and to create his own city fire department. I rose to the occasion to inform him of the importance of consolidation—the saved expenses to our citizens and the how this split would affect our fire department personnel. He stated that his motive was to demoralize the Township and to have them annexed into the city.

This was not a comfortable meeting for me, and the next day, I informed my superiors of the mayor's intentions. This goes to show that everyone in the political arena, city and township, had a motive for their existence. They all experienced egotistical issues and hoped that I would just climb on board.

There are three types of people: people who make things happen, people who watch things happen, and people who ask what happened. In my opinion, hard work and perseverance do pay off; however, you have to remember that when you are up to your elbows in alligators, it is important to recognize the main goal is to "drain the swamp." Even though Packer Township and Throop City have many alligators, I knew I could improve service, remain loyal to my township, and keep moving the organization forward. Kelvin Cochran, past United States fire administrator, makes a clear and profound statement. He states:

> *Like every other profession, we in the fire service suffer the embarrassment and damage to our hard earned reputation because of the very few who choose to break the law or rules. While that may be unfair, it is our reality in today's world of instant, mass communication.*

The Fire Service Reputation Management white paper clearly identifies these individuals and behaviors in a clear and cogent manner, articulates some excellent solutions, and clamors for a code of ethics as the next logical step for our profession. "We may never have the opportunity again, and I urge all fire service leaders to develop, establish, disseminate, abide, and enforce a Fire Service Code of Ethics."

CHAPTER 4
Strategic Analysis and Proposed Master Plan

"The beatings will continue until morale improves."
—Richard Peter Graywater

Convincing administrator Peter Graywater that we need to develop a strategic analysis and master plan was not an easy task. On a number of occasions, Graywater stated to me that he would rather run the firefighters into the ground with overtime than to perform a study. As time progressed, the career personnel felt used, and rightly so.

Firefighter/paramedic Buster Meyer often expressed a positive attitude in the direction our organization was heading and would frequently express his displeasure in the Packer Township government officials. Anytime Buster was discussing the Packer Township administrators or elected officials, he would call it "the Packer Township Puzzle Palace." This behavior provided me some insight on how the firefighters felt about the Packer Township administration, and it was my job to help resolve past nefarious organizational behaviors.

One of the pressing issues is that we needed additional career personnel, and Peter Graywater wanted to work the existing personnel more. As time progressed, I was finally able to convince all parties involved to sit down and talk about the overtime issue with all of the responsible people present. Initially, Graywater was captivated by the negative behaviors of the captains and career personnel; he soon realized what I had been proposing was the right thing to do by hiring additional personnel and relieving the burden being placed upon the firefighters. After listening to the facts, Graywater and Frank Lynn decided to allow me to seek a strategic plan for the Fire Protection District. In this meeting, money (no surprise) became a pressing issue. The firefighters were seeking additional compensation, and after much deliberation, Peter Graywater finally agreed.

Timothy Brooks, one of the senior career firefighters, was often the subject of disciplinary action and controversy. Brooks is a close friend of Thomas Vandyke and Michael Clinton. Mark was at this meeting and participated in the monetary compensation conversation but obviously had no clue what was going on and agreed to a five-cent raise.

This issue later became a contention, as Timothy Brooks blamed me for not stepping up to get him more money—but it was he who agreed to the five-cent-per-hour raise and even shook Peter Graywater's hand over the deal. Captain Brandon Clinton rose to Brooks' defense and demanded that I go back to Graywater to get more money for Brooks and for him as well.

Once again, their narrow minds got the best of them. They just accepted an offer from the administrator, Peter Graywater, and once the figures set in to their belittling minds, they then realized that they had screwed themselves—and they wanted me to fix their dilemmas.

Meanwhile, the City of Throop, under the direction of the Throop police chief Randall Green, developed an action plan of their own, which would only open another single vehicle station to house an EMS paramedic unit. He submitted this plan to the city manager, council, and the mayor of the city of Throop.

It was noted that Police Chief Green had no idea of what elements must be taken into consideration like flashover, personnel needed to complete certain tasks like ventilation in a timely manner, fire attack, having a rapid intervention team, and a command staff to effectively perform the work required. His comment was that the city has no problem letting the buildings burn as long as we had an EMS unit available to save the voters.

Green further stated that the housing in the city of Throop was insured and to let the insurance company figure out the damage. This narrow-minded approach was one of the contributing issues that helped me be successful in getting Peter Graywater to authorize a strategic analysis and develop a master plan for improvement.

It is important to remember that the customer is internal and external—a concept Peter Graywater has a hard time grasping. Furthermore, the customer is the most important person. A customer is not dependent on us, but we on them. A customer is not an interruption of ours, but the purpose. A customer is a person who brings us what he or she wants. It is our job is to provide the highest-quality services with the resources available. As such, we developed and entertained a request for proposals (RFP) in seeking a consulting firm, specializing in township risk analysis and fire/EMS delivery, and chose to accept the proposal by Samuel Carson of Boston, who had a number of specialists on his staff, including Dr. Anthony Romano. Romano was the lead consultant on our project and met with the staff, firefighters, and elected officials on a number of occasions.

Study Background

The trustees of Packer Township, acting as the governing board of the Packer Township Fire Protection District, commissioned The Consulting Group to conduct a study of the fire, emergency medical, and rescue services provided to the township, including the city of Throop. This Summary of Findings and Recommendations highlights some of the major issues that require discussion.

The study, which focused on both short-term and long-term planning goals, conducted in March 2000, involved site visits by three principal consultants who interviewed department members and others and reviewed numerous reports and other documents. They used computerized mapping to illustrate response distances and times developing a series of computed maps to illustrate possible alternatives and a specific approach to consider.

One of our primary conclusions was that the most efficient and cost-effective fire protection structure is to have one department for the township and the city and to use a combination of full-time career, part-time, and on-call personnel. Additionally, given the level of growth and the risks consultants observed, the current level of services was not fully adequate.

A summary compared the existing resource base and deployment with what the consultants considered a higher (and more adequate) level of service-delivery resources and thus, an improved capability to protect lives and property. Recognizing that expenditures must be matched by tax revenues, any system improvement should be constructed in phased increments, building from the current service delivery level through three possible phases, with the third phase designed to provide adequate service delivery in the future.

Fire Department Background

The Packer Township Fire Protection District is located in Richmond County. The township and the city of Throop are experiencing periods of rapid growth. Although the current township population is approximately twenty-four thousand, the City's Master Plan anticipates the "build out" to continue for twenty to twenty-five years. This growth will increase the demand for fire and pre-hospital emergency medical care services.

The Fire Protection District currently provides diverse fire protection and emergency medical services from one fire station. This modern facility, constructed in 1992, housed the administrative offices, crew quarters, a four-bay apparatus area, and a combination training and facility room. The Packer Township Fire Protection District has evolved over the years from its original volunteer fire company under contract with local government to a district-governed organization. Financing is provided by fundraising events and a small fire tax levy. The department was typical of small, rural volunteer fire companies.

In 1987, a new fire levy was enacted, and basic ambulance services were upgraded to provide advanced life support by deploying one certified paramedic and one emergency medical technician per unit. In August 1988, Packer Township assumed the responsibility for fire and EMS services under a fire chief who reports to the assistant township administrator, Frank Lynn. This evolution resulted in the volunteer personnel becoming part-time employees to staff duty crews and on-call assignments.

During 1992, several career positions were established. A paid fire chief replaced the volunteer chief, and a new facility was constructed. Over the years, internal changes occurred slowly and infrequently in the district, with the normal level of resistance one expects in traditional fire organizations. In 1997, a new fire chief was appointed, accelerating the pace of change within the department. Accountability and performance levels were established along with standard operating procedures.

The rapid implementation of needed changes resulted in serious organizational problems. Although the changes provided structure, discipline, and clearer direction, they inspired resistance from some members.

Principal Components of a Fire and Rescue System

The key components of fire suppression, emergency medical service delivery, technical rescue operations (vehicle wrecks, machinery accidents, trench collapses, etc.), and large-scale incident/disaster response depend on the number of trained responders immediately available, the time it takes for them to be summoned and respond to the scene, and the vehicles and equipment available to responders.

Legal requirements (most often related to responder safety) and the Insurance Services Office (ISO) evaluations of local fire protection for insurance premium purposes are important considerations. Moreover, national and industry standards are typically drawn from the National Fire Protection Association, the American Medical Association, the American Heart Association, and the Federal Emergency Management Agency and provide guidance for developing a response system. The standards for emergency medical response to life-threatening situations, for example, call for basic life-support measures to begin within four minutes, followed by advanced life-support measures within eight minutes.

For planning purposes, it is important to recognize that in typical residential fires, where most fire deaths happen, "flashover" occurs within eight to ten minutes. Therefore, for emergency medical, fire, and rescue calls, trained, certified responders should reach the scene in as close to four minutes as possible, with the full assignment of responders arriving within eight minutes.

Our application of benchmarks and standards to the Packer Township Fire Protection District shows that the existing single fire/EMS/rescue station is not sufficient to provide timely response throughout the district's service area. Computed response mapping, however, illustrates that a three-station configuration would likely provide coverage within four minutes' running time for about 80 percent of the district's roadways, assuming a forty-mile-per-hour average speed. The geographic area covered in a three-station configuration should account for about 90 percent of the annual total emergency calls.

Since total response time includes alarm and dispatch (national average of one minute), response crew reacting to the call and departing the station (one-minute average), and running (or "road") time, a four-minute running time is actually a six-minute response time. If responders are not in the station when the alarm sounds, the total response time is delayed substantially. In-station responders, whether full-time or part-time or volunteers working in the station, are essential to satisfy EMS and fire-suppression benchmarks and standards.

Sound practice required that the initial-response crew for emergency medical calls must be at least two certified responders and that the initial response crew for structural fire suppression should be a least four persons.

Without four people at the scene, the OSHA two-in/two-out rule (requirement for a minimum of four equipped personnel to be present before entry in a structure fire incident) presents operations problems and possible liability. Any sustained effort to augment initial response requires additional personnel to provide backup support.

Recommended System Improvements

The system calls for the alignment of three captain supervisors. The senior captain would serve as the director of operations, one captain would serve as the administration and information supervisor, and the third captain would be fire marshal. Each captain would also have a responsibility to serve as a night and weekend shift commander. Currently, the Packer Township Fire Protection District does not have sufficient personnel to provide even partially adequate staffing for fire suppression or advanced life-support services, nor is it staffed to handle frequent simultaneous calls.

The number of paramedics is depleted; the number of people available "within five minutes of the station" has diminished seriously; and the number of part-time employees available for shift work is dangerously low. The department has experienced and is experiencing personnel turnover that must be addressed. The limited economy and the tight employment market are factors that affect district employment. To improve recruitment and retention efforts and ensure greater employee participation, the following actions are emphasized by this study and have been introduced by the chief during the course of the study:

- The fire chief should place a stronger emphasis on the recruitment and retention of personnel.
- The fire chief should continue and be encouraged to continue to engage in efforts to keep personnel informed and solicit ideas from personnel within the department as well as from outside sources.

- Continue with periodic meetings with personnel, office meetings, and department-wide meetings.

The department should create standing committees covering five areas of concern:
- Part-time and "on-call volunteer" recruitment and retention
- Internal communication and newsletter
- Training and safety
- Target pre-planning
- Long-range planning

As the number of fire stations increases and the department expands to meet the needs of its service area, additional budget items are needed for equipment and the replacement of selected items. Moreover, the operating budget will increase substantially, requiring and additional tax levy.

Over the past several years, the department has become more modernized, more in keeping with district needs, and has improved in many respects. However, a higher level of capability and service delivery is needed for Packer Township and the city of Throop.

At this time, budget support, organizational morale, and internal dialogue and communication need improvement as part of a plan to enhance the effectiveness of the department. Part of any improvement plan should also provide for additional apparatus, employment of a fire marshal/inspector and a training/safety officer, and switching to the county dispatch system to enhance mutual aid.

Organization

Because the department is a small, combination organization that deploys a limited staff of seven career and uniformed personnel, supplemented by part-time, in-station, and on-call members, the structure is very basic. The fire chief serves as the chief executive officer (CEO) and delegates operational, support, and administrative responsibilities between two career captains. The career firefighter/paramedics and the part-time lieutenants share additional areas of responsibility. A physician is the non-paid medical director, who provides oversight of EMS functions; a part-time administrative assistant provides office support for the command personnel. Both of these positions report directly to the fire chief.

Limited staffing levels and priority for emergency-response demands affect the ability of the career fire captains to focus and manage their responsibility areas for inspections, prevention, training, scheduling, equipment, etc. Time management, availability, and task continuity all suffer in order to augment response staffing and provide emergency scene supervision. Under the current organization, personnel are supervised by part-time members every evening and during the entire weekend.

The Packer Township Fire Protection District has experienced a significant increase in demand for service. In 1990, the district responded to 682 calls for service; in 2000, it is estimated that the Fire Protection District will respond to 1,550 calls for service, a 127 percent increase over a ten-year period.

Staffing

The fire chief works normal business hours and employs a part-time administrative assistant. Two career fire captains work overlapping eight-hour shifts to provide weekday coverage from 0600 hours until 1800 hours. One career firefighter/paramedic is assigned to steady weekday work schedule from 0600 hours until 1800 hours with four part-time personnel. These on-duty members provide one paramedic engine company and one medic unit during weekday business hours.

One career firefighter/paramedic and two part-time personnel provide fire protection coverage (engine company) for evenings and weekends. Paid on-call personnel who respond from their location to the fire station upon notification provide EMS coverage during the same period.

The current system puts increased pressure on the career firefighter/paramedics that often serve multiple roles as the assigned officer, driver, and lead paramedic. In some instances, part-time lieutenants supervise career personnel.

The lack of adequate staffing, the complexities of a combination fire department, and the increasing need for career overtime shifts are having a debilitating effect on the department. Because of inadequate staffing, the philosophy is to respond to the fire emergency call first.

The initial engine (pumper) staffing is generally with three members and in some cases is accompanied by a medic unit with two personnel, depending on the day, time, and availability. In these instances, the Fire

Protection District can comply with the "two-in, two-out" standard recommended by the NFPA and OSHA. The Packer Township Fire Protection District is equipped with two front-line pumpers and three medic units, a brush fire unit, and a technical rescue truck.

Obtaining sufficient response personnel for an additional pumper and medic unit is difficult at times and may be delayed. The Fire Protection District is dependent on mutual aid to provide aerial apparatus support. Some of the existing industrial and commercial buildings and many of the newer residential properties are beyond the reach of thirty-five-foot ground ladders.

As the pool of available part-time fire personnel becomes smaller, many of the members willing to work are in danger of exceeding the hour limit established by law. Balancing this concern against the need to provide minimum staffing levels presents a difficult challenge for command personnel. Recruiting a sufficient number of new members from the immediate township is essential to meet part-time staffing requirements. This becomes more difficult, because the demographics of the current residents relocating into the new, upscale housing developments do not usually provide a pool of candidates for the fire service.

Apparatus

The Packer Township Fire Protection District deploys a modern, well-maintained fleet of emergency and support vehicles. The two pumpers are rated at 1,500 GPM, have large water tanks (750 gallons), and are both equipped with sufficient quantities of five-inch large-diameter hose line (LDH) for water supply and delivery. Each is also well equipped to provide necessary advanced life support services and fire-related operations.

All of the fleet meets or exceeds current apparatus/vehicle service life standards. The department does not have an aerial apparatus and relies on mutual aid from neighboring fire department to provide this support. To their credit, the members keep the apparatus in great condition. A private contractor (Fire Apparatus Service and Repair) who is a certified emergency vehicle technician (EVT) and an ASE-certified master mechanic provides preventive maintenance and repairs.

The fire apparatus maintenance personnel conducted annual pump testing and yearly safety inspections and provides input for new apparatus specifications. This current system is a cost-effective choice for smaller fire departments and appears to provide excellent service to Packer Township and twenty-one other area jurisdictions.

Communications

Emergency communications, call-taking and the City of Throop Police Department from a small facility located within the Municipal Building provide dispatch for the Fire District. The City of Throop Communications Center utilizes an 800-MHz partially truncated system to dispatch police, fire, and EMS units.

The center contains two positions for call-taking and dispatch and is on the E-911 telephone system. Communications personnel are also responsible for all public inquiries and administrative calls for police personnel. Normal staffing for the eight-hour shifts can be one or two call-taker/dispatchers, depending on peak service demand calculations. When one-person staffing occurs, it can be difficult to handle the multiple tasks efficiently, particularly simultaneous emergency actions.

The CAD system does have flags and prompters for emergency medical responses, and the assigned personnel are emergency medical dispatch (EMD) trained. Currently, the system does not provide printouts of emergency dispatch data. Tone-activated voice pagers are used for personnel notifications, and Motorola portable radios (MT-2000s) are used for fire scene communications. These multiple-channel units are compatible with the surrounding jurisdictions.

The Packer Township Fire Protection District pays the City of Throop $15,000 per year to provide these communications services. A viable alternative to the current communication system, available at no cost to the department, is the Richmond County Communication system, which provides services to almost all public safety agencies in the county.

This modern Motorola ten-frequency system has eleven interchangeable call-taker/dispatch positions and is the county's E-911 answering point. Minimum on-duty staffing is one supervisor and four personnel. Alpha pagers are used for alerting personnel and providing dispatch information.

The existing four tactical channels are being expanded to six. In the near future, mobile data Terminals (MDTs) will be provided for all emergency vehicles that participate in the Richmond County system. APCO Institute guidelines and protocols are followed by supervisory and line personnel.

The Fire Protection District is unable to take full advantage of automatic mutual aid capabilities while operating under the City of Throop communication system. With the Richmond County system, automatic aid can be fully utilized.

Operations

The department provides a limited range of emergency and support activities. These services include fire suppression, prevention, investigation, inspection, public education, township outreach, advanced life support emergency medical services, technical rescue, and natural and other disaster mitigation. A regional team provides hazardous material incident interventions.

The department is equipped to provide fire suppression, related emergency interventions, and pre-hospital emergency medical care. Two front-line pumpers, three medic units, one technical rescue vehicle, and one brush truck provide modern, well-maintained tools and equipment. Aerial apparatus service responds from mutual aid fire companies.

The majority of department members are trained and certified at varying EMS levels to provide both basic and advanced life support, including defibrillation. The City of Throop Police Department and the Packer Township Police Department vehicles also carry automatic external defibrillators (AEDs), and the personnel have the appropriate training, including CPR.

The Packer Township Fire Protection District participates in a countywide written mutual aid agreement that appears to work effectively. Because of the size of many of the Richmond County fire departments, mutual aid is a regular necessity. During 1999, the Packer Township Fire Protection District received mutual aid for fifty-two fire-related events and twenty-two EMS emergencies. Conversely, they sent assistance to twenty-five fire operations and fifty-one EMS responses.

Normal dispatch protocol for a structure fire is two pumpers, one medic unit, and the technical rescue unit. The number of responding personnel varies, depending on time-of-day availability. During 1999, an average of seven and a half personnel responded to reported structure-fire alarms, which is less than the national standard of twelve personnel.

Emergency Medical Service

The Packer Township Fire Protection District provides advanced life support pre-hospital emergency medical care utilizing three medic units and one initial responding "Paramedic Engine Company." At least one member on each of the responding units is a certified paramedic. A medical director, who assists the department in this non-paid position, provides oversight. Emergency room coordinators at area hospitals and one of the career fire captains provide quality assurance.

The state determines additional regulations; state law regulates certifications and re-certifications. The Packer Township Fire Protection District generated revenue from an EMS third-party recovery program established on May 26, 1994. During the period from July 1, 1994 through December 31, 1999, the department generated approximately $803,819 from the program. A private contractor handles the recovery at a reasonable cost to the Fire Protection District.

Finances

The Packer Township Fire Protection District is funded by a property tax-based fire levy of $3.5 million ($1 million in 1981 and $2.5 million in 1987), plus third-party billing revenues. Due to state law, these revenues are static because taxes are not influenced by inflation or increasing property values. In 1999, the department generated approximately $1,120,000 in revenues. Personnel expenses accounted for approximately 67 percent of the FY '99 operating budget (including benefits).

Staffing expenses (excluding benefits) for FY 2000 are projected at $753,276. Due to personnel shortages, the $30,000 budgeted for overtime in 2000 will probably exceed $52,000. Since the operating budget for the Fire Protection District is considerably less than comparable jurisdictions within Richmond County, the department attempts to take advantage of grant-funding opportunities. A five-year spending plan for capital expenses has been developed for apparatus, facility, and equipment expenses. Currently, the Packer Township Tax District has no debts for any capital issues.

Training and Safety

Although the Packer Township Fire Protection District does not have a dedicated officer for training, written guidelines exist for both fire- and EMS-related monthly training guidelines and evolutions. Training opportunities would appear to be too infrequent to be fully effective. The department attempts to comply with annual standards for SCBA, blood-borne pathogens, hazardous materials, etc., and for all EMS recertification policies. Certified in-house instructors conduct a driver-training program.

Training program responsibilities are delegated to one of the career captains, who have a long list of other duties to perform. One area of concern appears to be an adequate level of incident command training for both the career firefighter/paramedics and the part-time lieutenants.

External training programs are available at the Richmond County Joint Vocational Training Center for fire and EMS programs. The department does have a core group of state-certified instructors who can assist the training initiative. The local college provides additional local educational opportunities, particularly for EMS requirements.

Although the Packer Township Fire Protection District does not have a safety officer, they have attempted to comply with generally expected standards. Station-wear, bunker gear, hoods, SCBA, and PASS devices are provided and meet national specifications. Portable radios are provided for each "riding" position, but members do not have individual SCBA masks.

The station is equipped with a heavy-duty gear dryer, a MAKO breathing-air compressor, and an SCBA maintenance facility for in-house service and repairs. The station does not have a pre-piped vehicle exhaust venting system but is equipped with sprinkler and fire-detection system for personnel safety. The apparatus is compliant with NFPA Standard 1500.

Information Management

The Fire Protection District has done an excellent job of taking advantage of technology to enhance their information-management capabilities. Personal computers are used effectively for data management, storage, statistical generation, report processing, etc. This includes employee information, training records, operational data, budget statistics, and emergency response information.

The system is used to produce the annual report, employee handbook, and general operating guidelines, which are all current and professionally written. It is also used effectively to communicate and keep all personnel apprised of department activities and policy changes.

Fire Prevention/Inspections/Investigations

Because there is no dedicated staff for this function, the Packer Township Fire Protection District delegates a minimum of responsibility to several of the career firefighter/paramedics. The program is very basic and consists of fire station visitations, limited school programs, Fire Prevention Week activities, and some group home inspections. The department has marginal involvement in pre-planning of target hazards.

Township outreach programs are conducted upon request but are basically infrequent and undirected. One of the career captains is assigned investigative responsibilities. He receives assistance from the fire marshal's office and an investigative team from Richmond County. Although this system appears to function effectively, it is not tested frequently due to the low number of "working" fires.

Because of the lack of a dedicated fire inspector, this is an area of serious deficiency in the Fire Protection District. One career captain is responsible for juggling this responsibility among many others, and the function and the township are not served well. The assigned officer is a state-certified fire inspector and is responsible for enforcing the state's fire-prevention code. State inspectors conduct some Life Safety Code (NFPA Standard 101) inspections. The Packer Township Fire Protection District participates in the National Fire Incident Reporting System.

Inspection responsibilities for the fire department include plans review, new construction, fire-system inspections, complaints, remodeling, hydrant locations, Knox Box installations and detection systems, annual inspections of selected hazard types, etc. The Packer Township Fire Protection District has a good working relationship with the City of Throop Building Department and their inspectors; however, the City is becoming increasingly concerned because of the District's inability to perform this critical function.

Although the Richmond County Building Officials' office is assisting the inspection process in the county proper, the City is having recurring problems with the Fire Protection District, particularly with delays occurring to issue certificates of occupancy and temporary certificates of occupancy, which require a signoff by the district inspector.

The City of Throop director of public works is extremely concerned about the lack of mandated annual inspections, code compliance, violations, and the turnaround time for plans review and occupancy certifications. The major building boom is in the city of Throop, which is expected to continue for many years, exacerbating this situation.

These overall issues were presented to the Packer Township board of trustees and to the City of Throop council, city manager, and mayor. Dr. Anthony Romano's presentation met with opposition, in that the communities within the city of Throop felt embarrassed that the township management was not forward-thinking before this analysis. They should have known that there were serious concerns, and did nothing about this—until now.

Once the elected officials agreed to move forward, Chief Kelly Daugherty asked that this action plan become memorialized in a resolution, which was ultimately passed. This strategic analysis and action plan became our vision for a safer township.

However, this venture had a number of obstacles, including having Brandon Clinton and his group of harmful followers derails our efforts. In fact, Kimberly and Ted Malcom, both Fire Protection District officers, placed a **VOTE NO** sign in their yard—and Ted Malcom was a full-time lieutenant with a neighboring fire department, just north of Packer Township. Only the Malcolm's know what their motives were, but it did not make sense to the twenty-five thousand citizens they are sworn to protect.

Today's emergency-services environment is marked by change, which is driven primarily by a number of forces: the changing nature of the workplace, group decision-making, technology, economic shocks, domestic and global competition, new social trends, and politics.

While all public- and private-sector businesses face various types of change, we must be concerned with change activities that are proactive, purposeful, intentional, and goal-oriented. Planned change seeks to improve the ability of the organization to adapt to changes in the environment—thus meeting the customer's expectations.

Experience has shown that organizations and their members typically resist change. In a sense, resistance is positive. This resistance can be overt, implicit, immediate, or deferred. Active resistance might include being critical, finding fault, ridiculing, appealing to fear, using facts selectively, and blaming, accusing, sabotaging, intimating, manipulating, distorting facts, blocking, undermining, starting rumors, and arguing.

Employees who engage in passive resistance might agree verbally but fail to follow through on a task, fail to implement the change at all, procrastinate, pretend ignorance, and fail to offer information, suggestions, help, or support, and if at all possible, stand by and watch the change fail. Sources of resistance are individual and organizational but may overlap, and the executive staff might include resisters.

Below are some reasons why individuals within organizations may resist change:

- Feeling out of control; uncertainty
- Lack of time to adjust; stress from change overload
- Defending status quo to save face
- Concerns about future competence
- Implications for personal plans; more work
- Past resentments; concerns about winners/losers
- Perceived breach of psychological contract
- Lack of clarity as to what is expected
- Belief that the change is wrong in some manner; clashes with values

All levels of leadership must realize that resistance to change is real, whether resistance is overt or covert. Managers who watch for signs of resistance and who are proactive in responding to them will be more likely to manage a change successfully.

When planning a change, outlining a plan to deal with the most likely types of resistance can be an important step to successful change. Unfortunately, in this case, the resisters utilized any unorthodox tactic possible to gain the attention of the elected officials. The inaction of the elected leaders has led to truculent behavior, which is contagious if not eliminated.

A fire chief can only follow directions from the appointed and elected leaders—but it is the appointed and elected leaders who must provide reciprocity and respect to their chosen fire service leader's adviser. Unfortunately, Packer Township lacks the confidence to do what is right. They are consistently looking out for their own best interest and not the interest of the community they serve.

Chapter 5
Vote as If Your Life Depends on It

"Instead of thinking about where you are, think about where you want to be. It takes twenty years of hard work to become an overnight success."
—*Diana Rankin*

Once the Packer Township board of trustees approved placing a fire levy on the ballot, we began working on the strategy of getting the levy passed. Pamphlet information and a PowerPoint presentation were developed to illustrate the dire circumstances we all were in, should we continue traveling down a path of destruction. Interestingly enough, we still had a number of individuals willing to sacrifice themselves to keep the organization the way it was and obstructing progress.

Brandon Clinton, the operations and support captain, decided to play a different game. Instead of being a proponent, he gathered the other career officers and firefighters and solicited union certification. Clinton was the second in command, and according to the statutory requirements of the revised code, he was not eligible for union representation, but the other officers and firefighters were. Therefore, he decided to file an unfair labor practice (ULP) with the Employee Relations Board and obtained union legal representation.

Brandon Clinton lost the first summary judgment—favoring management's side—and subsequently filed a second time. This time, the Employee Relations Board not only ruled in management's favor but also pointed out that the law would need to change before ever allowing a second-in-command in a collective-bargaining unit. In addition, the Employee Relations Board stated all of the other Packer Township firefighters, excluding this captain, could submit an application to be recognized. This disappointment and embarrassment to Brandon Clinton exasperated his frustration and campaigned against the fire levy.

From time to time, citizens of the township and vendors we work with would inform me of incidents where Brandon Clinton would vent his frustration. The owner of a fire-equipment company informed me in writing on February 12, 2001 that Clinton, while at a neighboring fire department, was telling their personnel that the Packer Township Fire Protection District was opposing the need for a fire levy because of the fire chief.

One day, my services were needed to participate on an EMS request. Unfortunately, my driver was Pyle Goddard. Once we arrived at the hospital with the patient, I recognized that Timothy Brooks was lying in one of the patient beds. I walked in to inquire what had happened to him.

He explained that he had a severe pain in his left side, and the physicians were unsure what it might be. I asked if this was an appendix issue, and he replied that it might be. He also stated that he was concerned about having to go through surgery and having a scar. I lifted my shirt, showed him my scar from my appendectomy, and told him that it was nothing. This inappropriate act sent Pyle Goddard and Timothy Brooks running to Brandon Clinton, which fueled the rumor mill.

Before you know it, the media was calling, trying to make a spectacle of this innocent situation, and the Packer Township Fire Company, a social group within the organization, lodged an unsigned letter of no-confidence to the trustees, urging the trustees to get rid of Chief Daugherty. Subsequently, an investigation was conducted. However, not everyone agreed with the menacing individuals within the fire department.

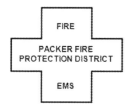

From:Firefighter John Chatman
Packer Township Fire Protection District

To President Clark Neil
Vice president Todd Lowe
Trustee Arthur Bode

I attended a meeting on October 30 of the Packer Township Volunteer Fire Club, and I disagree with a letter mailed by the Volunteer fire club to you, because of that meeting. The issue in disagreement was that of the leadership of Chief Kelly Daugherty. The correct information states as fact:
    11 No Confidence
    Eight Confidences
    5 Unmarked

Comments on the unmarked ballot include, refuse to vote, undecided, abstain
    Eleven people does NOT constitute a majority of the Fire Club. I personally was notified of this meeting just one day before the meeting was to take place and this did not provide all of the members to participate. I also believe that a number of members did not participate because of the single agenda—to vote no confidence on our fire chief.
    Several members at the meeting told me that within the past several weeks, telephone calls had been made and letters had been given by their lieutenants asking them to document any issue they feel needed to be addressed. The lieutenants said that the letters could be returned anonymously.
    A large number of the firefighters do not want to have anything to do with this quest of a few and we wanted to let you know. We support Chief Kelly Daugherty.

It has been the policy of the Packer Township Board of Trustees that complaints and compliments must be submitted in written form and signed; however, this policy also changes depending on the mood of the administrator, Peter Graywater, and chairman of the board.

According to the International Association of Fire Chiefs' "Fire Chief under Attack" publication, militant union officers are frequently inclined to use anti-management obstructionism to provoke controversy and create a platform for re-election. The IAFF leadership is accountable only to its members and to the mission of demonstrating a capacity for anti-management actions.

In pursuing the extreme, there is nothing to inhibit a local union or the "international" from using irresponsible and ruthless tactics. It is extremely difficult for an individual to match the resources of the IAFF in a legal battle or for a public official to win damages for defamation of character, invasion of privacy, or other intrusive and unethical acts.

The basic purpose of a labor organization is to enhance the compensation, benefits, and working conditions of its members through collective unity. The IAFF is composed of local unions, and the "international" exits primarily to support these locals. The IAFF enjoys strong public support and recognition, which plays a considerable role in the strategies of its local operation. The IAFF established a number of national-level objectives and uses the coordination between local and national offices to further those causes.

Conflict instigators are often backed by a minority of their local membership and by the resources of the headquarters staff, which included specialists in labor law and public relations. A press release from IAFF headquarters can add credibility to otherwise insignificant issues. Personal reputations are quickly damaged by the publication of biased reports in IAFF periodicals, which reach all the union members and a wide variety of interested individuals and organizations throughout North America.

The basic nature of a union organization, and of firefighters in particular, is to stand together in mutual support. This feeling is so strongly held that individual members will often go along with unethical tactics and actions, even if they disagree with the union position. A few radical individuals, like Brandon Clinton, who wanted badly to be in the union, can often sway the membership, particularly when they control the member's access to information.

Often, cases of anti-management action are initiated and successfully promoted by a small group of union members in an apparent attempt to promote their own personal agendas. There have been cases reported in which union officers developed such a strong personal desire to attack their chief that they violated rules of order and manipulated their own organization's bylaws to initiate official action.

Our plan was to deliver a consistent message throughout our township, in spite of the contaminated firefighters addressing only their concerns. It appears that Brandon Clinton, Thomas Vandyke, and others within their group were disappointed that I was able to ultimately deliver the "promise" to our township, when these individuals were spreading untruths and innuendo.

The passage of the fire levy was a huge issue, and a blow to its chances on passing came the week prior to the general election. The Richmond County auditor released property-valuation information, placing our fire levy in jeopardy. Unfortunately, the first attempt in passing the much-needed fire levy failed by twenty votes. The last time a fire levy was on the ballot was fourteen years previous. Soon after the official tally was posted, we began planning and re-introducing the fire levy for the second time. Fortunately, with this revaluation of the property tax, we were able to lower the millage of the fire levy, and in May 2001, we passed the fire levy with an overwhelming margin.

This impressive margin told us a number of things. First, the township understands the position of their fire/EMS department in the ability to meet the township's expectations. Second, they recognize that without key personnel available 24/7, their chances of survival and saving of their personal property were limited. Third, they recognized that the promise I had made to the township (not to come back to the township for additional funds for at least ten years), was something no one has ever presented. The township believed in my abilities and that I would deliver.

Soon after the passage of the fire levy, I found myself in an awkward situation. I was in the local grocery store, picking up some home items after work, when administrator Peter Graywater felt compelled to arbitrarily stick his wet finger in my right ear, twist it, and begin blowing kisses to my face.

Talk about a sick individual! Here, my supervisor, our township administrator, would lower his ethical values and moral standards so low that he felt it was appropriate that he embarrass me (and himself) in front of customers and residents with such an inappropriate act.

Now that the fire levy issue was behind us, and poised with a solid improvement plan for our township, firefighters from our organization and from throughout the state began lining up, seeking gainful, full-time employment. It appears that now that we had secured operational funding, everyone wanted to be my friend—including those individuals with the main goal of backstabbing me and wanting me fired! It is amazing that after I passed the fire levy, everyone now wanted to be my friend.

Kevin Dagg, one of our part-time firefighters, was also seeking full-time employment with the Fire Protection District. His father, Vincent Dagg, is the mayor for the city of Throop. Vincent Dagg and "Chairman" Clark Neil collaborated to get Kevin a job with the Fire Protection District.

Kevin Dagg is also a part-time police officer for the city of Austin and works part time for the US Marshals' office. Kevin had once tried to get a job with the City of Throop Police Department, but they would not hire him based on his past criminal history as a juvenile.

Kevin once told me that then-chief William MacNeil promised him a full-time firefighting job, but for some reason, Chief MacNeil stated that his "board" would not hire him. It is known that when Kevin Dagg was a juvenile, he racked up a criminal record, which is sealed.

Everyone who first saw me as a threat now wanted a job. Eric Brooks is the brother of Timothy Brooks, one of the Packer Township "Professional" Firefighters. Eric came to the Fire Protection District on the recommendation of his brother—and initially, had different characteristics than his brother. Timothy Brooks, on the other hand, is the type of person who gets upset over the fact that he felt that he should not have to take an assessment examination to obtain a supervisory position; it should be handed to him, since he has been with the fire department for a number of years.

One day, District Chief Michael Baum told me that when Timothy Brooks was hired, he was a close friend of Chief Thomas Vandyke—and before you know it, Timothy went from the last person on the hiring list to the first. Initially, I viewed Eric Brooks differently than his brother, displaying responsibility. However, this soon changed.

Firefighter Isaac Topper was hired a year before we embarked on the strategic plan and levy campaign, and for the most part, was a good employee. I did notice that Firefighter Topper was a little different from most of the firefighters—as if he had done something wrong and was hiding from something. As time progressed, it all started to make sense.

Richard Brice wanted a job very badly. In fact, one morning, I received a telephone call requesting Richard and his father to come visit me and talk about the fire service. The day Richard and his father walked into my office, I sensed that there was more to this story than I actually knew.

I listened as his father asked, "How does my son get into the fire service and become a firefighter/paramedic?"

My first question was "Why the fire service?"

The father replied, "My son wants to get into a profession, one which focuses on unity, teamwork, and trust." I was taken aback by these comments, but I also noted that they came from Richard's father—and not from Richard.

I was honored by Mr. Brice's views of the fire service and explained to him and his son that the first thing you need to do is to graduate from high school and then seek higher education. I also found out that Richard was a deviant in school, a person who would get into to a lot of trouble, and his father was trying to change Richard's behavior. Well, it appears that old habits are hard to break.

Another person who was part of the chief Thomas Vandyke/Captain Brandon Clinton malicious ensemble was James Pickings. James Pickings, at the time, was one of our part-time fire officers, who worked full time at neighboring fire department. James very much wanted to be part of our forward-thinking organization but had some serious past issues, which I objected to. I was told by Frank Lynn that Trustee Arthur Bode and Chairman of the Board Clark Neil wanted James Pickings to obtain a full-time job. However, before this was to occur, some "airing of the dirty laundry" needed to take place.

MEMORANDUM

TO Peter Graywater, Township Administrator
  FR: Frank Lynn, Assistant Administrator
  RE: Promotion & Last Chance Agreement for James Pickings
  DATE: July 11
  Cc: Kelly Daugherty, Fire Chief

On December 27, the Board promoted James Pickings to Acting Captain of Fire and Life Services as a part-time employee until the permanent funding was secured. The Board requested staff to obtain a written agreement known as a Last Chance Agreement from our labor attorney before any permanent full-time appointment was made and that this agreement had to be executed. The administrative staff is requesting to promote Mr. James Pickings at the next Trustees' Meeting with his first day being set for August. The proposed agreement is attached for your review and/or comments.

Bringing you and the Board of Trustees back up to speed with this request, in December the concern was James Pickings past drug usage. In the course of our Background check, his use of drugs came to light. During his polygraph session with Sergeant Oscar Day, Polygraphist, James Pickings gave the following admissions:

Applicant advises the following drug usage:

- *Applicant states he first used marijuana at age 11 and used it until '92 or '93.*
- *Applicant states that he last used marijuana on April 7 2000 at a concert.*
- *Applicant state that he has bought marijuana, had it given to him and has sold it.*
- *Applicant first stated that he had not sold marijuana then stated that he may have sold some joints.*
- *Applicant states that he in 1986 he used marijuana 2–3 times a month, 1985 to 1988 about 4 times a week and then from 1988–1992 less than 15 times total.*
- *Applicant states that he used speed when playing football in high school. He states they were called white crosses.*
- *Applicant states that he took a Valium that was not prescribed to him in 1995 before he took a plane trip.*
- *Applicant states that he used cocaine from 1985 to 1987 for a total of less than 5 times.*
- *Applicant states that he used LSD from age 18 till age 23 for a total of less than 5 times.*
- *Applicant state that he thinks he used a Quaalude one time.*
- *Applicant states that he snorted RUSH in High School*

(amylbuty.nitrate). In 1993 took a purple football (Xanax) at a party.

- *Applicant states that he used Hash about four times between the ages of 16 and 18.*
- *Applicant states that he smoked a marijuana cigarette 2–3 times laced with Opium.*
- *Applicant states that he used mushrooms in 1986–1987 about 3 times.*
- *Applicant states that he rides motorcycles with his buddies who take along drugs and use them on their outings.*
- *Applicant states that he was with them last weekend and he did not see any but was sure that some of them had drugs.*
- *Applicant states he has been trying to move away from being around drugs.*
- *Applicant states that he has seen some of his buddies with as much as ½ pound of marijuana.*
- *Applicant states that he has driven DUI before the last time being in September after a football game.*
- *Applicant states that in the first two to three years while working for Packer Township, he responded to call under the influence of alcohol and/or drugs.*
- *Applicant states, "I should not have been there."*
- *Applicant was asked what the worst thing was that we would find out about him, and he stated it would be his drug use.*
- *Applicant states that he has made some bad decision about it and can't handle it on his own and that is why church is his support now. Again, he stated he was not strong enough to handle this on his own.*

After the review of the polygraph, Township's staff required James Pickings to undergo a complete fit for duty assessment. In their assessment, they state, "It does not appear that placement in a formal drug and alcohol treatment program is indicated at this time."

I am requesting an executive session for the Trustees' Meeting to discuss the proposed appointment as well as the Last Chance Agreement.

It is unbelievable to me and to others that the Packer Township board of trustees actually hired and promoted James Pickings to the rank of captain.

It would appear that interpersonal dynamic issues with James Pickings have just begun. In fact, James Pickings has been counseled on a number of occasions, including misrepresenting himself as the fire chief when conducting fire and life safety inspections, conducting himself inappropriately with citizens concerning fire lane issues, and needing interpersonal dynamic and conflict-resolution training.

One such incident occurred when a businesswoman, holding and carrying her small child, was removing merchandise from her vehicle and bringing the items into her business. She was harassed by James Pickings for temporarily parking in a fire lane.

Instead of helping the businessperson, thus remedying the issue, James Pickings found it more important to harass and degrade the person. In fact, this person wrote a five-page complaint, which was sent to the City of Throop and to the Packer Township board of trustees. Ultimately, the Packer Township board of trustees backed James Pickings by allowing him to make this personal and public attack and did not seek a civilized resolution.

Pickings' inappropriate behavior has been documented on emergency calls as well. His presentation during a structure fire at a local chemical plant was unbecoming of an officer, when he wanted to "take control" of an interior operation from an equally qualified and ranked officer. It is apparent that the Gordon Personality Index previously administered would have validity in James Pickings's behavior.

Fortunately, these issues came to a head when administrator Peter Graywater began receiving complaints about Pickings' behavior—with some of those complaints coming from the Packer Township board of trustees.

Peter Graywater even called James to his office, informing him that it is not a matter of *if* but of *when* he would be relieved of his duties. This never occurred, because the Packer Township board of trustee members (Arthur Bode and Clark Neil) wanted James to keep his job.

It never fails to amaze me the lengths people will go to benefit themselves. Here we have a group of individuals who, for the most part, have their careers before them. The opportunities to do great things await them; however, they would rather take the low road and fabricate plans that fit their agendas. What ever happened to an honest day's wage for an honest day's work? Then it dawned on me—all of these individuals are around the same age and had lived or worked within our township for years. This common dominator led me to the generation of the millennials.

Today, the millennials are of the marrying age. In order to best serve this new group of twenty-something's, it is important to understand where they are coming from. Millennials have a strong bond with the technological age. They were practically born with a mouse in their hands and understand text messaging and instant messaging better than many of us understand how to e-mail.

With their ease around a keyboard, they have a different mentality about interacting with people and within their relationships. In general, the millennials want to be heard and to share their ideas, want to be involved in every aspect of a project, and view maintaining contact as essential—but not via phone or face-to-face meetings. Text messaging and e-mails are the preferred means for communication. You cannot put out a fire or save a life with a text message!

As a result of their communication styles, there is a higher expectation for an immediate response. Their "what's in it for me" mentality drives them to seek *their* kind of justice. Without meeting *their* expectation, they will do whatever is necessary to get what they want. This is critical information for any supervisor or manager to learn how these individuals think, act, and respond.

CHAPTER 6
Building, Growing and Anticipation

*"There are no secrets to success. Do not waste
your time looking for them. Success is the result of
perfection, hard work, learning from failure, loyalty
to those for whom you work and persistence"*
—*General Colin Powell*

The people of Throop and Packer Township had spoken, and now, with the passage of the fire levy, I was in position to implement what the citizens of our township supported—our master plan. One of the first orders of business was to design two user-friendly fire stations while keeping a keen eye on fiscal responsibilities. With Peter Graywater's approval, I wrote a request for proposal seeking an architect and engineering firm to participate in determining how we can best design our two new fire stations and provide construction management assistance.

It was obvious to me that Peter Graywater already had his favorite architect and engineering firm in mind, long before I placed pen to paper. Graywater was currently utilizing this firm with the Peachtree Park design. Mrs. Peachtree was a resident of Packer Township, and upon her death, she donated a large parcel of land to Packer Township and a million dollars to boot. Graywater had no problem spending other people's money—to the point that he actually ran out of money long before the entire project could be built.

As such, I soon found myself pinned between both the administrator, Peter Graywater, and the assistant township administrator, Frank Lynn. Graywater did not want Lynn to be involved in the fire station projects—which made me feel uncomfortable. This posturing on Graywater's part was primarily because Lynn did nothing to support the fire levy and that both individuals were at each other's throats on how to run the government center operations. One would tell the citizens and employees one thing, while the other would do the opposite.

Peter Graywater, a cigarette smoker, would require Lynn to enforce the no-smoking policy, while Graywater would run behind the road maintenance garage building to "catch a smoke." Graywater would rather sit and play on the computer in his office than participate in attending regional or statewide township meetings or even learn the latest laws and how they affect our organization. When asked to participate, he would state that he has an assistant township administrator, Frank Lynn, to take care of the human-resource stuff; he is too busy.

As we began building, staffing, and anticipating our future, I can only thank our township for providing me this opportunity in truly making a difference. While the department's naysayers were continually plotting devious events against me, I kept my focus on the citizens, our service delivery, and the opportunities I had been able to generate, based on the community's input.

Just as every fire chief must make decisions on the fire ground, the fire chief must make sound decisions on financial stability in order to secure success. Planning helps the organization by causing its employees to think ahead and anticipate change. This change begins with a clear mission for the organization that represents its reason for existence. Strategic plans translate the mission into a systems approach, designed to help accomplish the mission. Strategic plans set the organization's long-term direction.

As the fire chief, I was the principal architect in developing and implementing a strategic and master-planning process. As a result, a team of seventy highly skilled, combination career and part-time personnel were trained to meet the fire/EMS needs of our community.

This master-planning process included obtaining information from the stakeholders, both internally and externally, and meeting nationally recognized standards. The funding medium was through a property tax, which our citizens ultimately approved. Through appropriate strategic planning, we were able to increase staffing, build two additional fire/EMS stations, and recommend for purchase the necessary apparatus and equipment—all under budget.

It was my responsibility, as the chief financial officer for the fire department, to ensure that all aspects of budgeting and overall finance were appropriate and met guidelines established by the state auditor.

Salaries and benefits for career and part-time employees dominated my operating budget. I would review my budget monthly and reference it from previous years, based on generally accepted accounting principles.

I always took into account any unexpected issues that may arise throughout the course of the year. I am proud to say that over the past eleven years, even with increased demands by our firefighters to spend more, I was able to keep the fire department operating budget balanced, accurate, and meeting both the administrators' and organizational expectations.

Financial management is one area in which most chief fire executives have the least experience. I have embraced this challenge for our organization's benefit. I had been asked by a number of universities and our fire chiefs association to write a graduate-level public-sector finance program, designed to assist those command officers to better understand the budgetary process and instill a systems approach, utilized by the local government. This approach allows chief fire executives to capitalize on financial stability, efficiency, and overall organizational effectiveness.

As the fire chief, I was a visible township leader. The role is synonymous with integrity, honesty, and having high-quality communications skills. The fire chief is the principal agent, overseeing the day-to-day operations, and must have exemplary visionary and networking skills. As such, I, as the fire chief, am a leader, mentor, coach, and manager, with the ability to interact with the various individuals and departments, seeking ways to work in harmony for the stakeholders.

Fire-service leaders must understand that empowering employees is vital for organizational success. My philosophy is to have everyone in the fire department be responsible for important areas and provide them the tools and knowledge necessary so they may achieve their portion of organizational success.

I have enacted this practice for a number of years and have been able to build pride, confidence, and self-esteem in our personnel. It is important, however, that the right person is appropriately aligned for the project or task. The best indicator is to ask individuals what their special interests are and lead them in meeting collective goals. Items and issues I often reflect upon with our personnel include:

Setting the example: Modeling strong work habits through efficient, dedicated work practices. Let your own approach to daily work be an example from which employees can learn.

Communicating expectations: Communicate the job standards and expectations to the employees working for you. One cannot assume that these are self-evident to the employees, even though they may seem obvious to you.

Implementation of training program: Take time to train your employees in important work skills, attitudes, and habits, such as time management, telephone skills, customer service, and how to handle difficult situations.

Give feedback: Provide consistent and appropriate feedback to your employees. Employees benefit from feedback on job performance.

Establish and communicate policies: Establish internal policies to ensure that employees understand the rules, including those for absenteeism, tardiness, breaks, and dress codes.

Develop and maintain good relationships: Develop good supervisor/employee relations with the employees. This is not intended to be an intimate friendship but should be an association based on mutual trust, respect for each other, and a genuine interest in meeting the goals of the employee and the department.

Be flexible: Understand that employees are employees first and friends or family members second. Though it is important to have high standards on the job, it is also important to be flexible to individual obligations.

Give recognition: When you see an employee going the extra mile or persevering through difficult situations, acknowledge this in front of other staff and peers. People need to feel appreciated.

Share the vision: Have regular staff meetings with your employees, and inform them how their work fits into the larger purpose of the department and institution. Remember purposeful work is meaningful work.

Evaluate performance: Evaluate employee work performance as required, using realistic expectations. Employee accomplishments should be recognized as well as deficits. Use the evaluation to provide feedback to the employee about his or her performance.

Motivate workers: Motivate the employee to do the best job possible and to inspire both quality and quantity of work.

Discipline: Correct unacceptable behavior early, in private; describe the unacceptable behavior, the impact on the organization and other members, and give examples of proper action or behavior. Document everything.

One of our larger concerns, now that the organization was growing, was to have appropriate supervision on each shift and at each fire station. About this same time, trustee Arthur Bode was up for re-election and was beginning to feel the township heat (and from other candidates) on why the Fire Protection District had so much carryover funding. About this time, we were carrying forward around 7 million dollars; however, these funds were appropriately identified for when the revenue did not cover the anticipated operating expenses. This is a common and legal practice.

Peter Graywater approached me regarding this concern and told me to develop a plan to spend more money. I told him that I refused to spend the taxpayers' hard-earned dollars over some political rival; however, we did have a growing personnel problem, in that we no longer had enough creditable supervisors on each shift and at each of the three fire stations. Graywater ordered me to develop a plan to meet this demand.

I did develop a comprehensive, detailed plan to address the lack of supervision. Graywater felt that this was a pressing issue and called Chairman Clark Neil at his office to make a sales pitch. Little did I know that Graywater was using this as an alternative in solving trustee Arthur Bodes's dilemma. This is a deceitful way to help both the Fire Protection District and a seated political candidate. While this plan was appropriate for our organizational setting, it demanded an additional $900,000 annual requirement, which we had in reserve.

I was told to address this plan to Chairman Neil, and in turn, Neil called trustee Arthur Bode that he had some good news in helping him get the heat off his back and to help him get re-elected. Neil also told Graywater and Bode to meet before the next trustees meeting, in Peter Graywater's office, to inform Bode and Lowe how this plan would work and that Neil will make a motion to approve the plan, with Bode and Lowe affirming it in a general meeting.

This is only one example where Graywater, Neil, Lowe, and Bode held a private meeting right before the biweekly board of trustees meeting. While this technically is a violation of the ethics law, no one would ever cross Chairman Clark Neil. If you did, you would soon be out of a job.

To add insult to injury, about nine months after receiving permission to begin the process of hiring additional supervisors, Graywater told me that I needed to explain to the board of trustees what the value-added benefits were for increasing the Fire Protection District's budget. It was obvious that Graywater wanted to use me as his scapegoat when additional questions arose from the competing candidates vying for Bodes's trustee position.

As time progressed, I found myself being nominated for a Richmond County award by our shift captains. I was quite surprised in their letter addressed to the committee on how well my efforts had been perceived. Here is their letter of support.

Barber Redman Awards Selection Committee
  Captains Kevin Dagg, Tracy Blackman, and Dale McKee
  Nomination for Outstanding Service

We would like to nominate Fire Chief Kelly Daugherty for the outstanding service award. Chief Kelly Daugherty has been with Packer Fire Protection District for over ten years and he has done many things to completely revamp the department.

Chief Kelly Daugherty came to Packer Township when it was a volunteer fire department. He changed the staffing so that is now a fully staffed full time and part time fire department. Current staffing levels are at thirteen per day with plans to go to eighteen per day before year's end.

Chief Kelly Daugherty has made sure that the Fire District has the equipment and apparatus it needs to provide the best service to the citizens. We staff three medics, three engines, one ladder, one rescue, and one brush truck. We also have one reserve medic and one reserve engine in case of a problem with a first out engine or medic.

Since Chief Kelly Daugherty began reshaping our organization, it has gone from one fire station to three. Two outlying stations have a medic and an engine at each house. The main station has the remainder of the equipment as well as the reserve equipment. All three stations are staffed with ALS services at all times.

Chief Kelly Daugherty has created opportunities for people to fill many different ranks and to better themselves in their fire service careers. There are many part-time employees that have gotten their start at Packer Township or have come here after working at another job. Many people have gotten full time jobs at Packer Township with the expansion in staffing in the last several years.

These many staffing changes have also led to promotional opportunities for a number of people. There are five command staff positions that all have different responsibilities. Shift Lieutenant Positions were created and then Shift Captains were created with the addition of more Shift Lieutenants. These positions have given many personnel the opportunity to compete for positions and advance themselves.

Chief Kelly Daugherty is dedicated and loyal to the Packer Township Fire Protection District. He makes himself available all hours and days of the week. Even when he is out of town, he is available by telephone or email. He is also involved with committees and organizations at the county and state level. He has done things to help-out individuals, the Fire District, and other departments throughout our county and our State.

Because of the many things that Chief Kelly Daugherty has done for the Packer Township Fire Protection District, and the hard work and dedication that he has put into the Fire District, we feel that Chief Kelly Daugherty be recognized for outstanding service by receiving the "Barber Redman" award.

Equally surprising was a letter of my support to the elected officials by our Fire Union on how I take safety very seriously and was able to upgrade the firefighter's personal protective equipment, with the assistance of obtaining the Assistance to Firefighter's Grant through the Department of Homeland Security.

Packer Township Professional Firefighters
Chief Kelly Daugherty
As President of the Packer Township Professional Firefighters, I would like to commend you on the purchase and upgrade to our personal protective equipment. The members of the Packer Township Professional Firefighters will continue to strive for excellence while maintaining the highest level of safety.

The turnout gear purchase as well as the leather boots and rescue gloves will allow us to continue to serve the community safely and responsibly. We appreciate your diligence in making sure the members of the Packer Township Professional Firefighters are outfitted in the best possible gear.

Richard Brice, President
Packer Township Professional Firefighters

The person I recommended after Brandon Clinton had left the Fire Protection District to be our assistant chief was Mark Huston. Mark had been in the fire service for a number of years, mainly in the Pittsburg area. He too has witnessed a number of inappropriate firefighter behaviors, and for the most part, we carried the same set of ethics, morals, and values.

After five years on the job, Assistant Chief Mark Huston decided to leave Packer Township for a fire chief position. I supported Mark in his desire to help mold a struggling fire department and am proud of his accomplishments. While I do wish him well, Mark left without having any senior administrator speak to his new government council, and without writing a thank-you note to the Packer Township elected officials.

As time progressed, I was also able to meet the expectations of the master plan and those of our constituents. I was able to complete all of the recommendations, despite the confrontational and discourteous behavior of our personnel.

The following are the completed recommendations based on the Strategic Analysis and Master Plan

- Established a three-fire-station response model. The computer mapping in this report shows several generalized location models, which would improve response capability.
- Developed a plan for employing additional personnel. Ideally, in the long-term, the department should staff three stations. Seven personnel should be at Station 1, and three should be assigned to each of the two new fire stations.
- Personnel employed should be dual trained as firefighters and emergency medical personnel.
- Established minimum staffing levels based on a solid career in-station nucleus supplemented by on-call/part-time personnel.
- Added two additional fire stations—equipped with a paramedic engine company and a medic unit. A minimum of three qualified on-duty personnel should staff each new facility.
- Purchased a "Quint" type apparatus for the existing fire station. This unit can provide engine, EMS, and aerial service.
- Staffed the existing headquarters station in order to provide sufficient personnel for fire, EMS, and related emergencies.
- Provided consistent supervision for all shifts (shift captains and lieutenants).
- Created the position of captain, who also can serve as the training/safety officer.
- Created the position of fire marshal, responsible for inspections, prevention, and investigations.
- Developed a sound working relationship with the medical director to ensure effective service delivery.
- Became part of the Richmond County communications network. This is more cost-effective and much more efficient for fire/EMS emergencies.
- Developed an NFPA standard 1500 compliance plan (safety).
- Provided individual SCBA masks.
- Established a system for increased employee input and

participation in policy development (Packer Township Fire Protection District involvement).
- Provided off-duty team-building opportunities.
- Continued to consider employee concerns and morale.

All of the recommendations outlined are from Dr. Anthony Romano's Strategic Analysis and Master Plan and have been accomplished within a reasonable timeframe. The unfortunate part is, when I wanted to bring back Dr. Anthony Romano for a re-assessment, Peter Graywater felt otherwise.

I was then asked by the chairman of the board, Clark Neil, about our future outlook. I had the chance—this time at a public meeting—to gain Graywater's attention, in that we must have a review of our status by Dr. Anthony Romano, and to begin developing our next strategic plan.

Chairman Neil agreed, but "President" Peter Graywater was not too happy with me, insinuating that I broke ranks and talked directly to the chairman. I was only addressing a question Chairman Neil presented to me. Graywater has a long-standing order that *no one* is allowed to talk to any of the trustees unless Graywater authorizes you to proceed.

As for our organization, I came upon a motor vehicle accident one day, where a young person had inadvertently hit a pop-up trailer with her vehicle, leaving her trapped and unresponsive. The patient's facial features were destroyed by the impact of a metal object entering the windshield, damaging her face and airway.

Firefighter/paramedic Carl Eastman, secretary of the Packer Township Firefighters Union, responded from the closest station and had made two attempts to intubate the patient, succeeding on the second attempt. It took three attempts to establish an IV, the fourth attempt being successful. Even with all of the confusion, mainly caused by the onlookers, we all performed as a team.

I was very impressed by how well fire management and labor worked for the common good. This information was presented to EMS coordinator Darrell Short, who sent a report of our activities to the College of Emergency Physicians. As such, we were awarded the "Star of Life" for extraordinary efforts in successfully reviving a non-breathing patient resulting from a traumatic event. With such recognition, I felt that communications between labor and management reached a higher plateau. Little did I know that a turn of events was only months away.

Richmond County Hospital & Trauma Center
   Star of Life Awards Committee,

A 23-year-old female white patient was a driver of a motor vehicle crash in which the patient sustained significant facial trauma. The soft tissue injuries included a soft palate laceration, multiple cheek lacerations, and arterial bleeding from a lacerated external carotid artery. The patient also had multiple mid-face fractures, all of which made orotracheal intubation extremely difficult. The patient easily could have required a surgical airway.

   The skill demonstrated by the EMS crew from Packer Township that evening in expeditiously securing the airway enable the trauma team at Richmond County Hospital to quickly resuscitate and get the patient to angiography for embolization of the arterial bleeding is nothing short of heroic.

   Without a doubt, the quick action on the part of the pre-hospital medical team not only saved the life of this patient, but prevented anoxic brain injury. It is my privilege to work with such a top-notch medical team who warrants consideration of the Star of Life Award.
   Sincerely
   James Tractor, MD
   Assistant Director of Trauma
   Richmond County Hospital & Trauma Center

It would appear that the board of trustees appreciates my hard work! However, when it comes to facing the naysayers—where is the respect and loyalty for a hard worker with a strong work ethic?

Dear Chief Kelly Daugherty,

   We believe you can take great pride in the performance of the Packer Township Fire Protection District at the "Virginia Western" propane leak. While you were out of town, the district delivered a top shelf performance in a difficult situation. We are sure you know that Trustee Todd Lowe and Administrator Graywater were present at the command post and that Frank Lynn monitored the incident via radio. Their reports of the performance of the Fire Protection District are full of praise.

   We appreciate that the Packer Township Fire Protection District leadership has accepted the responsibility to train and prepare for incidents like this one. The advantages of the work both the Police and Fire Districts have done to preplan with the companies who operate within the so-called "Virginia Western" complex was obvious in the way last Friday's leak was handled the mutual expectations already established allowed the incident to be managed professionally and efficiently from the very beginning. Nice work!

We request that you forward our appreciation to all Packer Township Fire Protection District personnel for a job well done. We are pleased and proud that all Fire personnel understood and accepted their role in an incident of the magnitude. You have all shown the Packer Township Fire Protection District to be competent and professional. Thank you for a sparkling performance!

Respectfully,
    Trustee President Clark Neil
    Trustee Vice President Todd Lowe
    Trustee Arthur Bode

Here is what our schools have to say about my unwavering leadership:

Fire Chief Kelly Daugherty, Packer Township Fire Protection District

    As the school year ends, I would like to send a note thanking you and your staff for all of the great service that you provide to the Richmond County Career Center. It is a comfort to know that we have quick and efficient emergency services for our school. Every one of your medics that respond here impressed me with their positive attitudes in caring for our students and staff. Not every one of our calls are "true emergencies," but you would not know that from how professional and kind your staff is. Thanks again for the great service you provide us.

Sincerely,
    Alberta Lucia R.N., B.S.N, School Nurse/Safety Officer

However, with the good must come the bad. One of our firefighters was Pyle Goddard. Goddard is somewhat of a loner, and really did not interact with other firefighters. He was considerably older than the rest of the group and did not have commonality with most of the other firefighters.

District Chief Michael Baum told me that when Pyle Goddard was a fire officer (under the former fire chief), another Packer Township fire officer, who is still active, had an affair with Pyle's wife. One would think that if this had occurred, you would renounce your friend—but not Pyle. He divorced his wife and embraced his male friend. To me, something here is not right.

As time progressed, Pyle Goddard racked up a number of safety infractions. Pyle, who lived near the main station, would run to the station when we were dispatched to a structure fire or other serious event.

Pyle was told on a number of occasions never to run, but he would disregard his supervisor's orders and do whatever he wanted. It became clear that Goddard's behavior was becoming an increased risk to the Fire Protection District, his fellow firefighters, and the township.

Listed are some of the infractions made by Pyle Goddard:

- Failure to observe district rules and regulations
- Failure to carry out Fire Protection District policies and regulations
- Failure to report incident of concern to a supervisor
- Failure to report accidents, injuries, or equipment damage
- Disrespectful behavior to the fire chief
- Creating or contributing to unsanitary or unsafe conditions
- Failure to disinfect the medic unit after runs
- Neglect or carelessness in observance of official safety rules
- Conduct that may injure individuals
- Unsatisfactory work performance

Pyle Goddard had a history of being disrespectful, discourteous, and outright unreliable to do the right thing. As the fire chief, in my opinion, Pyle Goddard was a liability, and as time progressed, it became clear on how much liability he would bring to the citizens of the city of Throop and Packer Township.

Chapter 7
No Good Deed Goes Unpunished

"Bad faith likes discourse on friendship and loyalty"
—Mason Cooley

Long before Richard Brice became the president of the Packer Township Firefighters Union, I would hold a meeting every other month with our union officers to discuss items of importance as well as safety-related issues. As time progressed, Richard Brice became the new union president, and in the beginning, we shared an amicable relationship.

At our meetings, we would discuss a myriad of issues, including equipment purchases, response protocols, and even financial issues; however, at no time had there ever been any issues brought to our attention regarding flagrant safety violations or any major concerns. For the most part, we had a system in place, and everything was working fine.

As fire chief, it is my responsibility to assist others in meeting their goals. I want everyone to succeed and know that they have a genuine role in our organization. Administrator Peter Graywater and his sidekick, Frank Lynn, often told never to help the union—*they alone* would take care of that.

One day, my wife and I were at the local YMCA exercising in the early evening, and I spotted Lawrence Gray, the township's labor attorney, exercising on the stationary bicycle. My wife and I decided to walk over and say hi to Larry. Before we knew it, we were talking about everything—our township, our children, how everything was going, and I felt quite proud of our firefighters' accomplishments as a whole.

We then starting talking about labor/management issues, and I told Larry that I was quite proud of Richard Brice stepping up to the plate and being the leader for the firefighters. Larry told me that Richard Brice was a weak individual (from the labor/management negotiation meetings) and had people, like Pyle Goddard, pushing Kevin Dagg's agenda—and to be careful.

I reiterated to Larry that I had a good feeling that Richard Brice would not be swayed, and Larry's reply was, "No good deed goes unpunished." I did not think much of his comment at the time, but I sure found out what he was talking about over the next few months.

No matter how hard I worked for the firefighters and officers, they were still not appreciative of the fact that they could not run the organization by themselves. It takes an experienced and educated individual to be able to stand in front of the citizens and honestly explain to them what we do and how well we do it. One of the positions we were fortunate to obtain was a training and safety officer. The job requires an individual with a temperament compatible with leadership. The person holding this position must possess loyalty and integrity beyond reproach and demonstrate well-developed interpersonal management skills, be mature, sensitive, tactful, and comfortable with an organization in dynamic change.

Our training officer is also the township safety officer for all of the township employees. One of this person's roles is to keep us up to date with the Worker's Compensation laws. Patrick Jackson was the safety officer and reported the township safety issues to Frank Lynn, the assistant township administrator and me.

As time passed, Patrick Jackson got frustrated in dealing with Frank Lynn. One reason is that Frank Lynn mumbles and does not speak clearly and concisely. Another issue Patrick Jackson had is that he thinks he knows more than Frank Lynn, who had been taking care of the Worker's Compensation issues for the previous two decades. To add insult to injury, our training and safety officer, Patrick Jackson, was involved in a rear-end collision in his staff vehicle with another vehicle.

Jackson was on his cell phone while driving, talking to a non-public-safety person and hit the vehicle stopped at a traffic light in front of him. It is clear that Patrick Jackson did not exercise full situational awareness while operating the taxpayers' equipment, and in fact, he cause us embarrassment, and the repair cost was over $3,500, paid for by the taxpayers. Fortunately, the City of Throop police officer *did* ticket Jackson for failure to assure a clear distance. The Packer Township administrators did nothing.

Another role in our organization is the position of shift captain. According to the Packer Township Fire Protection District guidelines, the person holding this position shall possess loyalty and integrity beyond reproach and demonstrate well-developed interpersonal management skills and shall display maturity, sensitivity, tactfulness, and comfort with an organization in dynamic change. The shift captain shall accept responsibility, persuade and motivate employees and the public, and make sound judgments and decisions. The job demands an ability to perform under strenuous and stressful conditions at emergency incidents and under the constant stress of managerial responsibility.

One day, shift captain Tracy Blackman decided to let his better judgment be compromised by allowing the driver/operator of a fire engine that was experiencing mechanical failure to drive the engine back to the station. This act resulted in Blackman willfully neglecting and abusing fire department equipment. The operator of the vehicle begged Blackman to call a tow truck to bring the engine back to the station, but Blackman insisted that the operator drive the vehicle back.

In discussing this incident to administrator Peter Graywater, he told me to tell Blackman that if it was up to him, he would "fire the bastard" for damaging the fire engine. He further stated that, "There is no reason why these bastards cannot start taking care of the equipment. These engines are not cheap." The overall cost to the taxpayer was over $24,000 to replace the motor to the fire engine.

Peter Graywater told me to tell Tracy Blackman that he was on the verge of being demoted and that Captain Tracy Blackman's response would dictate if Graywater was going to demote him back to firefighter, instead of to the rank of lieutenant.

Firefighter Kevin Dagg appeared to be a bright young man, but as time passed, our assistant chief, Mark Huston, would come to know Kevin Dagg as a procrastinator, a union man, a person only out for himself, and a person who would get others to perform the work but take all of the credit. In my opinion, Kevin Dagg was lazy and had others do his dirty work.

Assistant Chief Huston often said that when the "kids" were out of line or when something went wrong, this place was like the old TV series *Peyton Place*—but in his terms, he would say, "As the fireplug turns"—meaning one negative thing after another. Some of the issues he was talking about included a firefighter losing a drug bag with morphine in it, like the past training Captain David Burke did, and backing up a fire engine without a backer or guide like a number of firefighters did, and resulting in property damage.

It makes you wonder if these people ever grow up. Assistant Chief Huston had a talent for evaluating people. He would often tell me that Kevin Dagg is someone you cannot trust. He would say that Dagg comes with a "silver spoon," and expects to be treated differently because his daddy is the mayor. Sure enough, as soon as Kevin became full time and passed his probationary period, he convinced the full-time firefighters to unionize.

I had no problem with the organization unionizing, but the township administrators and elected officials had a very hard time with this. The issue that disappointed me is that Kevin Dagg told me the firefighters wanted to unionize, not because of anything we (fire management), or I (the fire chief), had done wrong. His reason to unionize was to have status in the fire service and to get the union stickers for our cars.

This tactic is used by police and firefighters so when their "brothers" (meaning police officers) see the IAFF sticker on a vehicle making some type of infraction, they would probably not issue a ticket. What a lame excuse.

I suggested to Kevin Dagg that they might want to look at our career standard operational procedure for the basis of the union contract, but that advice were ignored. Kevin Dagg pushed to have union recognition but failed to follow the existing benefits. As such, the Packer Township firefighters were forced to follow the Federal Fair Labor Standards Act, which meant that overtime would not be awarded unless they accrued 212 hours of work in a 28-day work period.

This document was signed and agreed upon by Kevin Dagg, the Packer Township firefighters' original union representative. The sad part was that this act screwed the firefighters out of overtime. Previously, our agreement was to pay overtime anytime they worked over their scheduled shift. Once again, Kevin Dagg blamed me for his inability to think.

Assistant Chief Mark Huston told me on a number of occasions that Kevin Dagg has issues with authority. He does not like being wrong and wants to portray an image for the firefighters to follow. The problem I see is that Kevin Dagg does not have the maturity or experience and may never gain an honest level of command presence with this type of behavior.

The IAFC "Fire Chief under Attack" article illustrates that the political arena presents a different situation for many fire chiefs. The elected officials who ultimately determine the fate of most fire chiefs are extremely hard to predict; hence, the fire chief must be aware of the individual priorities and concerns of elected officials and must strive to maintain credibility with them. In many cases, the fire chief's access to elected officials is very limited, particularly under a city management system, whereas the union has free access and numerous ways to become involved in directly supporting or opposing candidates.

The union representatives can make false accusations to destroy the chief's credibility or promise to support a candidate in return for a vote against the fire chief. One of the union's goals in attacking the chief is to bypass the fire department's administrative system and deal directly with the local government, elected officials, and the media. Once the union can deal directly with the government, it can effectively lobby for implementation of labor interest, using popular public support as leverage against the elected official.

The question is how far the politicians will allow themselves to be manipulated and where their perceptions of the issues will lead. It is difficult to accept that an elected official may be more attracted to the votes and support that the union may promise to deliver than to the plans and policies of a conscientious fire chief who is interested in improving efficiency.

Kevin Dagg has a number of infractions listed in his personnel fire. On one occasion, he was upset that the Packer Township Government Center information technology administrator, Robert Burger, found that Dagg was soliciting and influencing other firefighters with pornographic material through the e-mail system, during work hours. Yes, the mayor's son did indeed send pornographic material in the township-wide e-mail system. Kevin Dagg received discipline and was held accountable for his actions, but he also held this against me, stating that I "should be protecting the firefighters from the township administrators." This is definitely the wrong attitude and choice of words for a firefighter—and more as a supervisor to use.

Anytime we needed to call the medical helicopter from the county hospital, Kevin Dagg would often comment on the female flight nurses, stating, "Man, I would love to get in your jumpsuit and have my way with that." I often told Dagg, "This behavior from a mid-level supervisor/officer and family man is unacceptable." Dagg would snicker and move on.

Dagg would always be present when any of "his people"—the firefighters—was in trouble. He even represented one of our firefighters who attempted suicide, and Dagg wanted him to keep his job. The board of trustees felt otherwise.

To my amazement, Throop residents found a video on YouTube of Packer Township firefighters sliding down the metal stairs in the apparatus bay on a backboard. This behavior must be eliminated; however, our Packer Township elected officials must have felt otherwise—since most of the negative firefighters still have a job.

The video is found at *www.youtube.com/watch?v=1r9Q0rm0Ibc*.

It was recorded and posted by Jack Brooks, firefighter Timothy Brooks' son. Jack was also one of the Packer Township firefighters and sought a full-time job with the Garland County Fire and Rescue Department. It is hard to say if Jack Brooks, his father Timothy, and his uncle Eric Brooks, are still sliding down stairs of fire stations with lifesaving EMS equipment our citizens rely upon.

I asked a number of fire and emergency-service individuals to comment on this video. I asked them to speak of integrity, ethics, and character and asked, "Are we losing our moral compass?" Some of their answers follow:

First of all, this would be considered horseplay at work and if one of them is injured while horseplay, the taxpayers would have to fork out the money. This is an issue of what is right and wrong.

The officer must likely knows that it is wrong but when your living at a station, some boredom might kick in. In addition, if this is being allowed at the station, what other ethical issues might be going on.

Based on the short video, all I can say is wow. This goes beyond a bored firefighter. The fireman are paid by the state/county/taxpayers and the equipment is paid for by taxpayers. He did not show great ethics in his decision to use medical equipment as a toy to slide down the stairs. Bored or not, this is unethical. What if he would have gotten hurt or the board would have gotten broken. It is taxpayer money that has to replace it and if he is injured on the job, it could end up with worker's compensation. Cannot really judge his total character other than to say he does not really think before he acts otherwise he would have thought about what he was doing and realized it was not a good idea. Especially since it was being recorded! Firefighters are looked up to by the public and really should think about what they do before they do it. With the internet and You Tube, it's bound to get out

I agree with you 100%. These days people are idiots, especially if they video tape it and put it on You Tube. You know they had to think in the back of their mind that this is probably not a good idea.

The saying "boys will be boys" can only forgive so much. What I see going on in this video is a blatant disregard of equipment, with at least two, possibly more, firefighters who didn't step up to say something is wrong here. One can only speculate if this was accomplished during shift hours or not, so I cannot argue that point, but the fact of the matter is these men have taken life saving equipment and put it in jeopardy.

A backboard is a pinnacle piece of evacuation equipment, which can seriously reduce the risks or further neck or back injury. By carelessly putting a 180-pound plus individual on it and riding it down a flight of stairs like a bobsled, this board could have been extremely damaged, even if not to the naked eye.

Picture the scenario of hauling a 350-pound man down a flight of stairs in an emergency when the board suddenly cracks and has him tumbling, as well as the rescue workers down to the bottom.

This to me is the equivalent of trying to smash your body armor plates with a hammer just to see if it would make a dent. There is never a time and a place for shenanigans in the fire station. Messing around with equipment that will probably be used within the next few days to help save lives, is simply intolerable.

These fire fighters are definitely in the wrong. They are not only putting their own well being in danger, but the act itself makes you wonder the level of professionalism in their fire house. There are several problems that could stem from this activity the first being a physical injury to the firefighter riding the board. This would lead to a shortage on the crew, lost productivity, possible rehab time, or even suspension of more than one firefighter.

This action could also cause the equipment they are using to malfunction when it is needed and the big question is, if these firefighters are engaging in this type of activity, what else might they be up to? Integrity; These firefighters do not know what integrity means.

Ethics; bottom line is that not only are they making themselves look like bad but they are making a bad name for all firefighters by doing such.

Character; they do not have any, or they would not have done what they did. Firefighters have people look at them like "that is what right looks like." The public puts firefighters/police officers up on a pedestal because they are supposed to have a higher standard than the rest of the public. Not in this case, not only have they embarrassed the company that they work for, but also they have embarrassed their last name.

Integrity (honor)—These people are paid with taxpayer's money.

Ethics (morals)—Is defined as the rules of conduct recognized in respect to a particular class of human actions or a particular group. This firefighter in the videos would not know anything about ethics, as recording things on video that are harmful to all firefighters.

Character (temperament)—Fire fighters are looked upon as people of courage and great wits about themselves, these are adults acting like kids.

Regardless if he is your supervisor, you must make the right choice and follow your ethical path. I believe that people that try to make others look bad are only in it for themselves. I too was in the service and there is no room for dishonesty. We rely on each other, which means following all orders.

Wow! The fact that the supervisors knew and did nothing is horrible. As a supervisor, I would not have allowed something like that to happen. Nevertheless, if it did, the participants would be punished by suspension for a couple of days. I definitely would make them remove that video. The existing supervisors need to be written-up at the very least.

If the public knew about this, especially the ones that are in the City of Throop, they would be disappointed in what their firefighters did. I think it would make them lose some respect for them. To the fellow firefighters that do have integrity, honesty and character, they should stand with their heads held high because they know that they would not do something like this nor take part in something like this. It just makes you look like idiots.

There is never a need to join the cause. We all must stand for ourselves and make the right decision on our own. The only person that we are hurting is ourselves. If someone asked of me to participate in such event, I would deny and walk away. It will always be hard when placed in a situation like that and others will push you into them. Let us not have peer pressure be our weak point.

"Union firefighters ... stick together in a show of solidarity, and it is generally accepted and understood that you will not be a whistle blower, turn-in or even testify against your fellow firefighter. If you do, you will be subject to ridicule, ostracized and generally ignored or blackballed."

One of the major issues often confronted is ensuring that our fire and EMS personnel have creditable and valid credentials. Eric Brooks, one of our career firefighter/paramedics, knowing the requirements set forth by the

Pennsylvania Department of Public Safety, Department of Emergency Medical Service, failed to maintain his paramedic certification.

In fact, Brooks went as far to say that he knew his paramedic card had expired and then lied about knowing that it was his responsibility to maintain it. His inaction permitted him to continue practicing as a paramedic, providing IV drugs and cardiac therapy, and then stated it was not his responsibility to keep track of his card—it was the Fire Protection District's responsibility.

This self-centered and pessimistic attitude on Brooks' part exposed the Fire Protection District to a very high risk of liability. We had to research each EMS run Eric Brooks was on, confront the patients, and confirm that no harm had been done. This level of risk also elevated our medical director's liability, since our medical director is the person signing off on the DEA-controlled drug license.

On a different occasion, our previous training captain had to find alternative employment after pissing off trustee Todd Lowe, past vice chairperson with the board of trustees. David Burke rented property from Lowe, and one day the straw broke the camel's back when Burke complained to Lowe over tenant/landlord issues.

Not too long after that, Lowe told me that he wanted David Burke fired. I told Lowe that the law for public employees is very different from the law for private-sector individuals—you simply cannot fire someone for pissing you off over a private matter. In an effort to cool both parties off, Burke and his family visited the local hotel one weekend to have a family getaway.

Burke soon found himself in trouble again, this time over a citizen complaint that they witnessed David Burke pulling his son, by the head (by both ears), out of his family car, and through a window.

A concerned citizen immediately called the police department, claiming child abuse. Burke soon found himself in deep trouble and called me once again to help him out. I always find it amazing that the firefighters would call me to help them out, but when it came time for them to fulfill their jobs—that request fell on deaf ears.

One evening, David Burke's wife came crying to my house, begging me to keep Burke employed. I told his wife, "You really need to be talking to your husband and not me." He had disrupted our organization to the point that the trustees no longer trusted him.

Burke never told his wife of his antics and behaviors that led him to be asked by the board of trustees to leave our organization.

One day during a paramedic refresher taught by nurses from the local hospital, with some of the female flight nurses present in the classroom, Richard Brice felt courageous and daring and burst out his version of a PowerPoint presentation on abnormal trauma injuries.

One particular slide illustrated a nude black male. Firefighter Richard Brice spoke of "pulling traction on the black box area" in reference to the man's genitals. This behavior is highly inappropriate, shameful, racist, and fractious, placing the Fire Protection District in a bad light.

To: File
From: Captain Dale Mckee
District Chief Michael Baum
Subject: Firefighter Richard Brice inappropriate comment during paramedic refresher class

The intention of this memo is to summarize the discussion I had with Firefighter Richard Brice about his inappropriate comment during the recent paramedic refresher class.

Firefighter Richard Brice made an inappropriate comment towards a picture of an injured patient that was nude which was displayed during a basic trauma life support lecture. Firefighter Brice commented about "pulling traction on the black box area" the area was the man's genitalia.

After the instructor placed the group on break, I spoke with Firefighter Richard Brice about his inappropriate comment. The comment to Firefighter Brice was humorous however; there were citizens in the classroom thus lowering the professionalism of our fire protection district personnel.

The unfortunate part is that firefighter Brice's supervisors only talked to him about this incident and did not follow up with a notice of infraction. This is how the firefighter "brothers" take care of one another. However, if this were a senior officer, paperwork would be flying off the shelf!

During the next year, we embarked on replacing the assistant chief position. The finalists were Michael Baum, the current district chief; Craig Rider from Georgia; Jimmy Johnson from Columbus, Indiana; and Chet Rhodes from New Mexico. I spoke with a number of people about the finalists—including Kevin Dagg, and he said that no one in the fire department respects District Chief Michael Baum, since all he does is sit in his office. Chet Rhodes was a good choice, but he was recently let go at the Career Center in Packer Township and did not make too many friends while he was the public safety coordinator. Jimmy Johnson lacked experience, and Craig Rider was rough.

It was interesting that when I would bring up Michael Baum's name in conversation, administrator Peter Graywater would state that he "would never promote Michael Baum." Apparently, District Chief Michael Baum had some run-in with Peter Graywater, and Graywater did not hold Michael Baum in high regard.

When it came time to replace the past assistant chief, after a lengthy selection process, Peter Graywater told me that I needed to make a recommendation. My recommendation was to investigate further the background of Craig Rider. Craig Rider lived in Georgia, and Peter Graywater and Frank Lynn stated that they would not support me in making the investigation trip. Instead, they recommend hiring him.

On the first day of Craig Rider's employment, I knew that the trustees and Graywater had made a huge mistake. Rider immediately came into the organization and told people he was here to *fix* the department. Over the first year, Rider did not make friends—including the trustees.

After Craig Rider's six-month evaluation, I informed Craig that he should consider doing the following:

- Start going to the board of trustees meetings
- Start teaching trainings once a month
- Get more involved during shift briefing
- Learn more about the people in our community
- Interact more with Trustee Bode and Trustee Neil
- Watch your language around people
- Start using our radio terminology
- Be more friendly
- Watch your audience—Craig Rider surrounds himself around individuals like him. He has not demonstrated abilities to think for himself

Since Craig's last evaluation (nine month), he has become more argumentative and arrogant toward me. In mid-February, Rider was given an order to work out a plan on how we can ensure the ladder truck being more available than it currently was.

Rider wrote a memo, which did not cover the goal, but then came into my office and wanted to argue with me about the ladder truck availability. I told Craig that his behavior was inappropriate, but he kept on with his argument.

Over time, I found Rider to be very disrespectful to me and other senior officials over an operational issue, which he should have knowledge in solving. This behavior exhibited by Craig Rider was inconsistent with a qualified assistant chief or second in charge.

Rider, after receiving a poor six-month evaluation and a marginal nine-month evaluation, traveled to all of the stations to win people over; however, he was not supportive of upper management and knew that two trustees did not care for his style of management.

In fact, trustees Arthur Bode and Ed Neil both called me to their offices and told me how displeased they were with Craig Rider—so displeased, I thought for sure that they were going to send him down the road with his bags packed. Overall, I found Craig Rider to be very short and evasive when asked specific questions.

Some of the other issues I presented to Peter Graywater regarding Craig Rider are:

- *In my opinion, Craig Rider is not prepared for our Monday morning command staff meetings.*
- *Craig Rider is not trustworthy. On a number of occasions, Craig Rider has not been available for major responses in our township, and when asked specific questions, he cannot look me straight in the eye and give me a straight answer.*
- *It appears that Craig Rider will do whatever he can to make himself appear that he is improving (six-month and nine-month evaluation periods) then begin to go downhill. His attitude toward the township, in my opinion, and me is inconsistent with what is expected of a senior officer.*
- *Craig Rider does not like to get too involved in EMS (he has told me so); he likes to make runs and stand around. His office is a mess, this after repeated times of me telling him to get organized.*
- *Craig Rider is a procrastinator—not taking the appropriate time to get his area of responsibilities completed in a timely manner.*
- *Craig Rider always has an excuse on what is taking him so long to complete a project.*

- *Craig Rider is not a paperwork type of person; however, this position demands it.*
- *Craig Rider's work ethic changed after his six-month review and again after his nine-month review—good for a few days, then back to the same evasive behavior.*
- *Craig Rider spends a great amount of time on the computer system—viewing issues in Georgia and the air force. (I told Craig a number of times that he needs to concentrate more on his work.)*
- *Craig Rider has a forceful personality about him—wanting to make jokes to get people to like him. Craig Rider presents more of a buddy to firefighters instead of setting the example and being a leader.*
- *Craig Rider has an air about himself, which I do not trust. We should be working very close, but I get the impression that Craig Rider will do whatever he needs—and not thinking about our relationship or that of the township.*
- *Craig Rider presents himself to me that he would fight for his people over protecting the interests of the township. After the Pyle Goddard incident, Craig Rider told me in a meeting that, "You should have let Pyle Goddard go and not interfered." I told him that that was the wrong approach—you have to look out for everyone's interest and protection all of the time.*
- *Craig Rider came into our organization and immediately made enemies, stating that he is here to change things— Craig Rider has not recovered from these behaviors, and if continued, will severely damage our organization and everything we worked to achieve.*

As previously identified, Assistant Chief Craig Rider has a number of years working in the fire service and in a military setting. While such distinction is admirable, there are situations where his presentation appears to be misinterpreted. Comments by other officers include:

- *Appears to be angry.*
- *Expectations of others are not clear.*
- *His experience, while good, is from a different setting; teaching and mentoring opportunities are limited.*
- *Become more proficient in our communication system;*

> *misses radio traffic from crews and/or the Richmond County Communications.*
> - *Presents a frustrated appearance when projects are delayed.*
> - *When referring to the Packer Township Fire Protection District, he has the demeanor that we have done things wrong in the past and he is going to teach us the right way to do things.*
> - *Overreacts to minor situations around the station—how will he handle a true emergency? A calm, focused command presence is required in this role at all times.*
> - *Interpersonal relations approach to personnel, situations, and citizens; need to be nicer, with an emphasis on courtesy.*

As with all new employees, Assistant Chief Rider did have some areas needing improvement. Rider needed to do a better job in keeping me more informed on day-to-day operations, issues with Fire Protection District personnel, ensuring that our employees meet qualifications (including driver training and pump operations) and paying closer attention to follow-up with our personnel. Do not assume that your directives will be completed; you are held responsible for their inaction.

Assistant Chief Rider has, on occasion, written directives and correspondences to Fire Protection District personnel; while his original correspondence is very short, his terminology (oral and written) is less than desirable.

With the number of years Rider has in writing correspondences in a military setting, this style is not conducive to our organization. I suggest Assistant Chief Rider review all of his communications and ensure that they are appropriately written, taking into consideration the setting in which we operate. This also applies to his verbal terminology.

Assistant Chief Rider had been corrected on a number of occasions on his terminology utilized on the fire ground. A seasoned individual would be able to decipher his intentions, while less-seasoned individuals are confused, which can lead to unexpected circumstances.

Some additional areas in which Assistant Chief Rider needed to improve included getting more involved with EMS activities, participating as a crew member from time to time, being cognizant of his candidness (unintentional comments may present a negative posture), being aware of how his actions are interpreted off-duty, especially in the presence of subordinate employees, and becoming more proficient in our incident-management system.

As time passed, both trustee Arthur Bode and trustee Clark Neil came to me and stated that they wanted Assistant Chief Craig Rider gone. The unfortunate part is that they kept him for an extended period of time, which created additional problems for our organization.

Meanwhile, firefighter Pyle Goddard continued to rack up a number of safety infractions and insubordination charges. It would appear that Goddard had an agenda, in that he was not going to be a team player, follow instructions, and be forward-thinking when it came to safety-related issues.

Goddard became an organizational liability with his inept behavior toward safety and working with others. Over the years, he racked up a number of safety and behavior-related infractions, which were identified and presented by most of the department supervisors.

Finally, it got to the point where Pyle needed to be sat down and these behavioral issues addressed. District Chief Michael Baum did meet with Goddard to outline what he identified as a "pattern of self-destructive behavior." Goddard did not want to see what was contained in his personnel file and resigned instead of conforming to our organizational values.

Pyle Goddard took his last parting shot at our organization in the form of his resignation letter:

To the Township Administration,

My endurance has come to an end. I can no longer endure being a target of unfair attention. I freely admit that I have performed deeds that were wrong. What I do not understand is why others perform the same deeds and no action is taken. I have told the truth each time.

I am under investigation at this point in time. When I questioned District Chief Michael Baum, I was told I had made myself a target. I questioned him as to the meaning of that term. He stated one reason was that my hesitancy concerning the health and wellness program.

I stated that Assistant Chief Huston had explained the program to me. I explained that I would not sign away my privacy rights. Assistant Chief Huston became upset and stated that the not signing issue would be handled at a later date. I took the physical being very careful concerning any paper I would sign. I was very disturbed to be called into a meeting requesting that I sign a paper agreeing to set a meeting with Fire District Physician, Dr. Bradley Moore.

The meeting was to discuss with Dr. Bradley Moore a problem the physical had detected. In the interim, I had made another appointment and another test performed. This properly performed retest showed nothing abnormal. I made my feeling quite clear as to how I would proceed. That being that Dr. Bradley Moore was not my doctor. He had no need for a meeting with me due to the face of the retest proved no abnormality. I questioned how my records had been released without my authorization. I received no answer. I had stated that I had no problem with the program. I merely desired answers as to who would set the standards. In addition, who would see the records?

This was but one of an unknown number of instances where by questioning I had made myself a target. I am also concerned with the many times command has placed civilians, police, and fire department personnel in danger. Firefighters have been taught, through never ending classes, the correct procedures to utilize at a scene. However, many times this training is overridden by command. One such instance I questioned why the scene was handled as it was, I was severely chastised and belittled. By not following training, personnel are, at times in limbo as to how to handle the situation and also please command. Sometimes nothing is done in order to not get into trouble.

Trust and respect are wonderful things. Both must be earned. No one can take these from a person. One must give them away. Also, these are not one way items. One must give to get. Honor and dignity are also good. My honor has held fairly firm. Through intimidation, I have allowed my dignity to sometime become tattered.

Fear and intimidation are not good management tools. This type of management has led to bad morale and job performance. Personal incentive, pride in oneself and the department suffer. The department has lost many good people due to this style of management. Caring, giving people who became disillusioned, and moved to other department or quit altogether.

Another item, which may see small, is the annual awards.

The decision of who deserved the awards was taken from the fellow workers. Who better to judge than those who work with the people? This action was viewed as a very hurtful thing.

Also the pop and the candy machines caused quite a deal. This action also led to bad morale. The Packer Township Fire Company investment money has led to some conversations.

I am quite disturbed that I have been lied to, lied about and been call a liar. It has been not only myself, but my friends that have been called liars. These remarks have been issued from the various levels of the organization.

I thank all people who have made it possible for me to serve the community these many years. I am very sorry for any troubles I have caused. I will accept no personal contact with any fire department administrative personnel in the future. Any questions will be handled by the mail service. I will not allow myself to become more upset that my present level of frustration.

It is with a heavy heart that I tender my resignation from the department. I know that if I would survive this onslaught that something else will, as in the past, be misinterpreted or I will have an occasion to make another mistake.

Pyle Goddard
P.S. "I don't remember doing it. But if I did, I'm sorry."

> *"Tyrants have always some slight shades of virtue;*
> *they support the laws before destroying them"*
> *-Voltaire*

Well, as fate would have it, Craig Rider's overall evaluations as an assistant chief and officer finally caught up with his antics. Rider was faced with either finding another job or being fired. He left to go back to Georgia. Rider and Goddard will not be missed. They both were a cancerous source in our organization, and they needed to move on.

If you can figure this resignation letter out, then you are a much better person than I. Since this information is public record, I asked a number of our personnel just exactly what did this mean? Kevin Dagg said, "Chief, you know Pyle Goddard; he never makes sense." I asked James Pickings his opinion, and Pickings just looked at the letter, looked at me funny, and then began shaking his head in disgust.

I also asked a psychologist friend of mine what he thought of Goddard's letter, and that person said Goddard is exhibiting signs of depression, paranoia, and schizophrenia. A number of people in our organization wondered about Goddard's ability to cope in a group setting and this letter serves as an example of his behavior and state of mind.

Along with these personnel issues, we were faced with negotiating a three-year contract with the labor union. Retired assistant chief James Downs of Fresno, California, said it best in the IAFC publication, "Fire Chief under Attack." He states, "It would have been advantageous to know in advance that such union actions were being taught in IAFF negotiations training. When such an action is not warranted and there has been virtually no basis, then such tactics come as a major surprise. It does cause public embarrassment and insult. When the local news media is hungry for headlines it is virtually impossible to reverse the personal and professional damage that is done."

The increasing tendency for local unions to initiate personal attacks against fire chiefs appears to be supported strategically by the International Association of Firefighters (IAFF) at the national level. The attacks are made on chiefs who are disliked by the union leadership for some particular reason and are used simply as part of an increasingly hostile anti-management strategy. In some areas, unwarranted actions against fire department chief officers have become so common that they appear to be a standard tactic in the collective bargaining process.

The fire chief is often severely limited in responding to the attacks, especially when compared to the ability of union members to initiate the attacks, which are subject to few restraints on their behavior and tactics. When the union attacks are successful, the chief may be dismissed or forced to resign and may have a difficult time finding employment as a fire chief in another jurisdiction.

The attempt to undermine the chief's personal and professional creditability within the political process, and through the news media, is often used in an effort to soften up management prior to contract negotiations. Often this tactic is used to resist the chief's efforts to implement changes in the department or as an attempt to oust the chief in favor of a candidate supported by the union. The issues behind the conflict are generally contrived or unusual situational factors, chosen specifically because the instigator knows that the "problem" is beyond the control of the fire chief.

It is important to note that in most cases, chiefs who observe the status quo almost never come into conflict, while chiefs who try to change the system for the better are attacked viciously and repeatedly. These attacks can be particularly destructive, as the progressive chief is likely to be highly dedicated to the mission and make a strong personal commitment to solving problems and improving conditions. If the union tactics are successful in causing the chief's dismissal or resignation, the IAFF may even go further to inhibit the individual's attempts to find a new job. This has been done through publicizing the conflict in areas where the chief seeks employment or by submitting motions of censure against the chief during the IAFF annual convention.

CHAPTER 8
Main Event

"If you tell the truth, you don't have to remember anything"
—*Mark Twain*

On February 14, 2008, I was returning to the fire station after doing a background check on an officer candidate. On the way back, I got a telephone call from Assistant Chief Craig Rider to find out when I would be back. I told him I was quite a distance away from the Fire Protection District. He wanted to take Fey Purdy, our administrative clerk, out for lunch. I told him that I would not be back in time, and he should go ahead to lunch without me.

By noon, I had returned to our jurisdiction, so I proceeded to my residence to have lunch with my wife. We often went home for lunch, since we lived close to both our places of employment. Just before I left home to go back to work, our department was dispatched to an EMS call at our main fire station. The backup medic unit was dispatched, as the primary medic unit was out on a previous EMS call. As I proceeded back, I met the backup medic unit passing my street. The backup medic unit was advised by Captain Dale McKee that the EMS call was for a non-breathing patient.

I decided to follow the backup medic unit, since I did not know if the person was one of our employees or not. (I was thinking that this could have been Fey, because she stated earlier that she was not feeling well.) I followed the backup medic unit to the rear of the fire station. Once we arrived, I stayed in my vehicle for a moment and observed what was going on.

I noticed that a past employee was delivering advanced life support on a patient, so I then decided to get out of my car to take a closer look.

Once I got to where the crew were, I noticed former firefighter Pyle Goddard and his son, Howard—both past fire department employees—who has no jurisdiction performing invasive maneuvers under our medical director's license and certification—was found inserting an IV tube in an IV bag and intubating the patient.

I leaned forward to take the IV equipment away from Pyle Goddard; however, he resisted, pulling away from me and yelling at me. I told Pyle that I cannot let him touch any of our equipment, for this was a liability issue to the Fire Protection District and our medical director, as Pyle and his son were no longer employees of the Township.

Pyle and Howard Goddard are citizens—not employees of the Fire Protection District. Howard Goddard is a firefighter with a fire department in a different county, but this does not give him the right to do whatever he pleases. Howard Goddard was able to obtain employment after he destroyed relationships with so many of the Packer Township firefighters and needed to leave the county, just to save face.

In our state, even if you have an active paramedic card, you are *not* permitted to practice your skills, unless the fire chief and the medical director authorize such activity. Howard Goddard violated state protocol and jeopardized our medical director's license. This behavior goes beyond being negative—it is negligent and irresponsible.

There may be an issue of trespassing and theft on Pyle and Howard Goddard's part as well. They should not have gotten involved—especially since the patient was a relative of theirs. Once I obtained the IV equipment from Pyle Goddard, I placed the equipment in the medic unit.

Pyle then told me that he knew this would happen someday—indicating that we had a reserve medic unit on station and we did not utilize this vehicle for the patient—his father. I did not know that the patient was his father; my focus was to let the medic and on-station crews do their job and to get Pyle and Howard Goddard away from them. After the run, I called Captain Dale McKee into my office and asked him what was going on.

Captain Mckee then told me that Howard Goddard would not get out of the crew's way, and Howard Goddard intubated the patient (his grandfather) himself. I told Captain McKee that he needed to make sure this information was documented on the EMS report. When the crew got back from the run, I called them to my office to discuss what had occurred. This is when Captain Mckee told me that Howard Goddard would not get out of the way, even after several repeated requests to do so by Captain McKee.

The official EMS report stated, "Howard Goddard, FF/EMT-P, is the patient's grandson and he insisted on intubating and would not move out of the way. Captain McKee could not remove him from patient care." Keep in mind that there were three certified and qualified paramedics at the station on scene when the patient came in. There was no reason for Howard Goddard to exert his positioning at this scene.

After this meeting, I immediately went to inform Assistant Township Administrator Frank Lynn of this incident. Lynn told me that the Goddard's should not have interfered and he did not feel that I had acted inappropriately—especially knowing that I was trying to protect the Township from any liability issues.

Frank Lynn told me to make sure the crew at the station documented this incident, in the event something would arise—but he did not feel it would. I then had the crew write this event up and place it in my mailbox.

Later that evening, there was a scheduled board of trustees meeting. After the meeting, outside the building, I informed trustees Todd Lowe and Clark Neil about what had occurred today.

Trustee Lowe told me that he did not like Pyle Goddard anyway and that family related him to the Goddard's. At this time, trustee Neil exited the building, I informed both trustees what had occurred today, and trustee Neil stated that he did not like Pyle and that I did the right thing.

I explained what I saw and what I did, and both trustees stated that I "did the right thing in protecting the Township from liability." Trustee Lowe then stated that anytime the EMS unit is called to his office, he would step back and let the crews do their job. Both trustees reiterated that I did what was right in protecting the Township and that Pyle and his son Howard were wrong. I also told them that they needed to know, in the event Pyle Goddard were to start anything. Sure enough—he did.

Our state law states that no person, without privilege to do so and with purpose to prevent, obstruct, or delay the performance by a public official of any authorized act within the public official's official capacity, shall do any act that hampers or impedes a public official in the performance of the public official's lawful duties. Whoever violates this section is guilty of obstructing official business.

Obstructing official business is a misdemeanor of the second degree. If a violation of this section creates a risk of physical harm to any person, obstructing official business is a felony of the fifth degree.

Assistant township administrator and safety director Frank Lynn is familiar with this section of the law (since he was a commissioned police officer) and did nothing about this. As such, and in accordance with the Packer Township regulations, Lynn was guilty of malfeasance (wrongdoing or misconduct, especially by a public official), misfeasance (the performance of a lawful action in an illegal or improper manner—not doing his job), nonfeasance (failure to act; *especially* failure to do what ought to be done), and neglect (implies giving insufficient attention to something that merits one's attention).

PACKER TOWNSHIP, RICHMOND COUNTY

In official action by the Board of Packer Township at a public meeting conducted herein:

OATH OF OFFICE

I, Frank Lynn, do solemnly swear that I will support the constitution of The United States and the state constitution, and that I will faithfully discharge the duties required as the Chief of Police and Police Constable for Packer Township Police Department of Packer Township, Richmond County, to which I have been appointed according to law and the best of my ability, during my continuance.

In testimony whereof, and witness by my signature

Packer Township Board of Trustees

In addition, Captain McKee failed to do his job as a supervisor. If he knew he was having difficulties with an irate family member, he should have called for a police officer to respond to the scene. In my opinion, had this been anyone other than the Goddard's, Captain McKee would have performed his job and protected the crew, protected the patient, and protect the Township from liability. Captain McKee failed to do his job.

As a result of this incident, Pyle and Howard Goddard sought the assistance of Richard Brice, the Packer Township Professional Firefighters president; Carl Eastman, the Packer Township Professional Firefighters secretary; and Captain Kevin Dagg, (the son of Vincent Dagg, mayor of the city of Throop). Captains McKee and Blackman (both shift captains) also solicited information from former fire chief Thomas Vandyke and others to develop a plan on how they would "get back at the chief" for doing his job and doing the right thing.

Russ Hamilton, a neighboring fire chief, then addressed the Richmond County Fire Chiefs Association and made sure that I, Chief Kelly Daugherty, would not be recognized for my hard work and providing leadership for City of Throop and Packer Township for the past twelve years. I received this information from President Richard Peter Graywater. It appears that Russ Hamilton had it in for Chief Kelly Daugherty and administrator Peter Graywater, stating to me on a number of occasions that he hates Peter Graywater for what he had done to past fire chief Thomas Vandyke.

Dealing with unselfish firefighters is one thing, but why do some "leaders" feel it is appropriate to kick a fellow fire chief? This question has plagued a number of fire chiefs after I informed them of what I was told Russ Hamilton had apparently done.

Kevin Dagg had told me on a number of occasions that he knows that Pyle Goddard is a screw-up, but he is also his friend. As friends, Kevin would do anything to help Pyle. Now it appears that Kevin Dagg would lie, cheat, and deceive others to reinforce his friendship with Pyle Goddard.

A reprimand from then-assistant chief Mark Huston stated that Pyle Goddard, when employed with the Fire Protection District, would go out of his way just to alienate the chief and start trouble. Pyle Goddard has a chip on his shoulder over an incident that occurred in early 2001, where he stated that he saw the chief display inappropriate behavior. This accusation was found not to be true, and when Assistant Chief Huston asked for specifics and names, Pyle Goddard stated, "I do not rat on my friends."

> *"A friend to all is a friend to none"*
> —*Benjamin Austin*

CHAPTER 9
Just the "Tip of the Iceberg," He Says...

"It is better to be quotable than to be honest."
—Craig Stoppard

A synopsis of the allegations logged by the Packer Township Professional Firefighters included inappropriate behavior at a paramedic refresher class, inappropriate comments at a blood drive, creating a hostile work environment, abuse of power, and "owning" individuals, interfering at an emergency scene, and overall having unrealistic expectations.

Subsequently, the Packer Township chairman of the board, Clark Neil, and the Packer Township board of trustees ordered the Packer Township police chief, John Prewer, to conduct an internal investigation. Past employee Brandon Clinton, one of the members in the audience, expressed concern, in that the police chief should *not* conduct the investigation, yet Chairman Neil stated that the police chief will conduct the investigation and that is that. Neil would later change his mind and have another outside person perform an investigation *after* the police chief completed the investigation. Talk about hypocrisy and playing the political field!

Richard Brice, president of the Packer Township Professional Firefighters, was interviewed by the local print and news media and kept saying, "This is just the tip of the iceberg." You have to love it when someone tries to make his or her point by saying "This is only the tip of the iceberg." Uneducated people use this slang when they are emphasizing a position, and it is usually not true.

The Merriam-Webster Dictionary defines "tip of the iceberg" as the earliest, most obvious, or most superficial manifestation of some phenomenon. It is obvious that the union president, Richard Brice, needed to find some catchy phrase to help build urgency to his point. The media loved this so much that they went so far as to camp a photographer outside of my home.

> *"Get your facts first, and then you can distort*
> *them as much as you please."*
> —Mark Twain

President Richard Brice wanted to point out that this situation was only the beginning; this was just a small indication of a larger problem. After obtaining depositions from most of the key players, we found that they manufactured the urgency and "did what they could," as stated by Secretary Carl Eastman. The Packer Township Firefighters Union, Captain Kevin Dagg, former fire chief Thomas Vandyke, former captain Brandon Clinton, and his spiteful group went to great lengths to have the media come to my home, intimidate my wife at our front door one evening, and try to spin the liberal side of the allegations to my family, friends, and township.

The media will do whatever they can to bring you the story, no matter the validity. It is true that the leftist media employ devious, sinister tactics and literally go on in-your-face missions to deceive and alter perceptions. You might ask yourself, "How and why does the media use scare tactics to portray potentially negative news?" The answer is because it works.

We all know that at times, the news is scary, but we watch it and react to it, some positively and others negatively; it is our choice. Think about this: if you were a reporter who wanted to get the best ratings, wouldn't you use the most powerful tool in the human experience? They do it because it works. If we did not react to negative and scary news so powerfully and predictably, they would not use it; but we do because we are human. It is a sad day when reporters cannot be truthful and creditable.

The professional firefighters placed lies in the local and international newspapers (and websites like the International Association of Firefighters and Fire Chiefs), all in an effort to discredit me. Meanwhile, a limited number of the firefighters would attend the biweekly board of trustees meetings, just to comment on my behavior and how I ran the Fire Protection District into the ground, according to them. This is typical behavior of a group of people wanting to have things change to their liking and not considering the customer.

On March 9, Richard Brice admitted in a deposition that he prepared an unqualified written complaint about Fire Chief Kelly Daugherty. He, as the firefighters' president, stated that through several years, "a lot of people had several things, you know, they were complaining about and had concerns about and it got to the point where people were tired of dealing with it, and tired of living in fear." How dramatic can a person be?

Richard Brice was asked by Chief Prewer, "Didn't you say that this had been going on for several years?" *Yes,* stated Brice. "Then do you have this documented or a file that you maintained relating to these concerns that were brought to your attention over several years?" Richard Brice replied that there is *no formal or informal file.* It appears that credibility is not part of Brice's vocabulary. He had ample help from Captain Kevin Dagg, who helped write the complaints. The complaints first addressed operational issues. *When Richard Brice realized that Bode and Lynn were not buying their story, they switched to inappropriate behavior statements.*

According to almost every dictionary, credibility refers to the objective and subjective components of the believability of a source or message. Traditionally, credibility has two key components: trustworthiness and expertise, which both have objective and subjective components.

Trustworthiness is based more on subjective factors, but can include objective measurements such as established reliability. Expertise can be similarly subjectively perceived but also includes relatively objective characteristics of the source or message (e.g., credentials, certification, or information quality). Credibility, whether testimony is worthy of belief, is based on competence of the witness and likelihood that it is true. Unless the testimony is contrary to other known facts or is extremely unlikely based on human experience, the test of credibility is purely subjective.

My attorney, Thomas Murtaugh asked Richard Brice, "So how did you put together all the information that you put in the written complaint that you submitted to the trustees?"

Richard Brice stated, "Because everyone is aware of what goes on in the firehouse. Everyone knows what people disagree with, what people do not like. People talk, but no one really wanted to do anything because the Township has a history of sweeping things under the rug, and no one wants to be called as the whistleblower."

Murtaugh asked, "The Township does, or Chief Kelly Daugherty specifically?"

Brice said, "Well, both."

Brice was asked, "Give me some examples. What do you mean by the Township sweeping things under the rug?"

Brice stated, "In 2001, the chief was accused of the same circumstances and only got sensitivity training." He went on to say, "So the same things went on for several more years. Therefore, who wants to bring things up and then have to deal with being the employee of scrutiny, and the Township does nothing about it. A lot of the times people would just deal with whatever they didn't like and move on."

Brice was then asked, "So from 2001 to 2008, are you aware of any complaints that were brought to the Township's attention concerning Chief Kelly Daugherty and the way he interacted with the fire staff?"

Brice said, "No, nobody filed formal complaints."

Murtaugh asked, "In that period of time, you are not aware of any complaints that were made?"

Brice stated, "Nothing formal."

Thomas Murtaugh asked, "And from the time that you began as president in 2005, you didn't prepare any sorts of grievances or any other documentation relating to concerns about how Chief Kelly Daugherty was conducting himself?"

Brice stated, "No. I mean the Labor Agreement was not violated, so there wouldn't be a grievance."

Murtaugh asked, "Are you saying that Chief Kelly Daugherty didn't do anything that you believe violated the contract?"

Brice stated, "As far as like the actual language of the contract, there were no formal grievances."

Murtaugh asked, "Do you believe his conduct violated any of the provisions of the contract?"

Brice stated, "Not to my knowledge."

Murtaugh asked, "Did you ever seek any advice from the Association of Professional Firefighters concerning someone else's opinion, whether the behavior that you are talking about violated any of the provisions contained in the contract?"

Brice stated, "Yes, I was in contact with the district vice president."

Murtaugh asked, "Did you share with him some of the complaints that you or other members of the union had about Chief Kelly Daugherty?"

Brice stated, "Yes."

Murtaugh then asked, "And what advice did he give you?"

Brice stated, "To talk to the weakest trustee and get this information filed as a complaint."

Murtaugh asked, "And did you follow that advice?"

Brice stated, "Yes."

Murtaugh asked, "When did you talk to the trustees?"

Brice stated, "I don't know the exact date, but I had dinner with Arthur Bode, who's the trustee, and Frank Lynn, who is the public safety director."

Murtaugh asked, "Is that the first time you brought those things to their attention?"

Brice stated, "Yes."

Murtaugh asked, "What was their response when you brought those concerns to their attention?"

Brice stated, "Frank Lynn told me to put everything in writing and have it on his desk Monday morning."

Carl Eastman lied when he stated in deposition that Frank Lynn told him and Richard Brice to submit their complaint anonymously. In fact, Frank Lynn stated, "I thought it was inappropriate for an employee to contact a trustee to make an arrangement," but did nothing to prevent this behavior.

One of the plausible reasons why the Packer Township Professional Firefighters pursued these issues is because the Packer Township "professional" trustee, Isaac Topper, was recently disciplined for failure to perform his job. Just before these accusations, our department was dispatched to a structure fire, and one of the career firefighter/ paramedics, Isaac Topper, while *on duty,* opted not to make the call. The situation occurred late in the afternoon. Isaac Topper did hear the dispatch and was attempting to get on the fire engine; however, he noticed his replacement driving down the street, turning into the fire station parking lot, and waited for this individual to enter the building. This delayed a fire engine by ten minutes to a structure fire call.

> *"Lack of loyalty is one of the major causes*
> *of failure in every walk of life."*
> —*Napoleon Hill*

Fire service employees take an oath of office stating that they will abide by the rules and regulations of the organization. Responding to emergencies in a timely manner is a critical aspect of our positions. Isaac Topper purposely waited for his replacement to enter the building and then asked if the other person would make the call for him. This resulted in a ten-minute delay in response by the engine company—not to mention the travel time it took to get to the structure fire. This individual failed to respond to an emergency and left work prior to the end of his shift without receiving prior authorization. This is a serious offense, and explaining this behavior to Isaac Topper and his immediate supervisor was challenging.

This situation resulted in Topper receiving discipline and an action plan for improved future performance. This did not sit well with Isaac Topper or the union. It appears that the union wants to change the rules when it is convenient for them. What about the customer—you know, the people who pay our salary? An apology is definitely in order, but as Pyle Goddard says, "I would never rat on my friends."

Previously, the Department of Safety was investigating Isaac Topper for a domestic violence complaint they had received. Topper came to me, begging me to help him clear his name so he could keep his fire/paramedic certifications—the portable credentials needed to perform as a firefighter/paramedic. Had I not placed a good word to the State regarding his character, Isaac Topper would have lost his license to practice and essentially been out of a job.

Police Chief John Prewer, in the course of his investigation, spoke with Isaac Topper. Topper stated that two summers ago, he was working on a building ventilation shaft and was on a ladder. He stated the chief wanted something done and started to climb the ladder. He states that he told the chief he would come down off the ladder, but the chief insisted on continuing up the ladder. He states that the chief came up from behind him on the ladder and began working on the project. He states that the chief leaned into him as both were working on the project. He states this went on for two to three minutes, with both of them doing the same thing. He states that other firefighters were making fun of him.

Police Chief Prewer asked Isaac Topper if he filed a complaint to anyone, and Topper stated that he didn't want to be retaliated against. Prewer then asked him if the chief, for anything he did wrong, had ever retaliated against him, and he stated, "No," and then added, "You can't take on Chief Kelly Daugherty one-on-one."

Prewer then said, "Give me an example of anyone you have seen the chief retaliate against."

Topper stated, "Pyle Goddard."

Prewer then asked him to give an example of when he saw the chief retaliate against Pyle Goddard, and he could not explain why he used this as an example.

Isaac Topper was asked to continue with further examples of retaliation, and it was found that the complainant could not give any examples. He then came back with, "Pyle Goddard was forced out," but when asked how, he could not explain.

Prewer asked Topper how the ladder event made him feel, and he originally stated "Uncomfortable." Later in the conversation, Topper changed this to, "He violated me." Prewer then asked the complainant to explain why he had changed his initial comment of, "It made me feel uncomfortable" to "He violated me." Prewer then asked Topper, "Well, what are you going to call it, uncomfortable or he violated me, because that's a big difference?"

Topper's demeanor then changed, and he barked, "He uncomfortably violated me." Topper stated that Captain McKee was present and observed this event. He stated neither he nor Captain McKee reported this event when it occurred.

Topper stated that he has seen Chief Kelly Daugherty tuck his shirt in three or four times in eight years. He stated this was in the bathroom but could not provide any dates. Prewer asked him if he felt this was directed as something sexual in nature, or was he just tucking his shirt in, and he stated, "I don't feel it was sexual in nature, just odd."

Prewer then asked Topper why everyone was coming forward now, and he stated, "The Goddard incident started it." *Isaac Topper, after being asked, stated that he was in on the meetings where creating the complaints against the chief was discussed.* Topper stated that he made it to two meetings that occurred discussing what to do. Topper states that Blackman, Dagg, Richard Brice, Eastman, and he were at the first meeting. Topper stated that at the second meeting, the following people were there: Pyle, Kaiser, Stearns, Ronald Parr, Timothy Brooks, William Estep, Jeff Fairchild, Richard Brice, Eastman, and himself.

Topper then stated that he remembers now that Timothy Brooks was retaliated against after the 2001 incident. Police Chief John Prewer asked him how he now remembered this, and he stated that the chief would call Timothy Brooks into his office.

Prewer asked Topper if he knew why the chief called Timothy Brooks in, and he stated "No." Prewer asked Topper how he knew it was retaliation, and he stated that Timothy Brooks would come out and state, "That's bullshit," quite a bit. He then admitted that he still did not know why Timothy Brooks called it that. (Note: Timothy Brooks did not mention or state that this happened in his interview.)

In regards to a hostile work environment/abuse of power, Isaac Topper states, "*This may sound petty, but the chief made us wash and wax the American Red Cross vehicle.*" When asked when this occurred, he stated, "Five years ago." I asked him if he did not like washing cars, and he stated, "On Fridays, this is part of what we have to do."

Isaac Topper stated that there are part-timers who have other professional talents, and the chief makes them build stuff and do other things other than be firefighters while they are working and that they had to use their own tools. Prewer asked Topper if they were not being paid while they were there, and he stated that it was abuse for these guys to have to do this.

Prewer asked Topper if anyone ever told the chief that they did not want to do this, and Topper stated that he did not know. Prewer asked Topper if he ever saw the chief going around and chewing people out in public, banging tables, yelling, etc., and Topper stated, "No."

Chief John Prewer also interviewed Captain Kevin Dagg, and Dagg stated that he has no personal complaint of improper touching or improper behavior. Captain Kevin Dagg stated that he had witnessed some events, like in 2006, he was there when the chief "grabbed" Luther Graf's butt.

Prewer asked, "How did he grab it?"

Captain Kevin Dagg stated the chief "aggressively grabbed Graf's butt." According to Chief Prewer, other firefighter statements contradict Captain Kevin Dagg's statement.

Captain Kevin Dagg stated the chief was doing the training, and it involved feeling down the patient's back. Captain Dagg stated that Luther Graf advised him that he did not want to do anything with this (meaning he did not want to make any complaint). Chief Prewer asked if the chief was joking when he did this, and Captain Dagg stated, "Could have been a joke; I don't know".

Captain Dagg stated that Captain James Pickings asked Luther Graf three times if he wanted to do anything with this. Captain Dagg stated that Graf did not want to "rock the boat."

In further questioning, Captain Dagg stated that a few months ago, the Township Blood Center was there for a blood drive. He stated that the chief was talking with the crew and made the comment, "You got cock on your breath." Captain Dagg stated, "I think he was trying to be funny, but it didn't work." Dagg stated that he wanted to add some new complaints. He stated when Lieutenant Robert Story was being hired, Chief Daugherty made a joke in front of Lieutenant Story and his wife about whether they were "going to get it on when I leave."

During Lieutenant Robert Story's interview, he described the event as the chief making a joke and stating, "She is going to have to beat you off with a stick tonight," not the statement Captain Dagg was giving as a complaint. Lieutenant Story stated that neither he nor his wife was offended about this event. *Lieutenant Robert Story stated in his interview that he feels as if the union on this issue is using him.* Lieutenant Story stated that he did not ask the union to bring this forward as a complaint. I am curious as to why Captain Dagg is trying to use this.

Captain Kevin Dagg was asked about a hostile work environment/ abuse of power. He provided examples of a training meeting. Captain Patrick Jackson brought up an idea, and Chief Daugherty went off on him in front of everybody. This was not identified in Captain Jackson's statement. Captain Dagg also stated that he has seen District Chief Michael Baum berated dozens of times, and Assistant Chief Craig Rider was berated every day. This, too, was not identified in either Assistant Chief Craig Rider or District Chief Michael Baum's statement. Captain Kevin Dagg states if any crew screwed up, everyone was then punished.

Captain Kevin Dagg states, Chief Daugherty and Captain Pickings had an argument over the hose drill at the high school. Captain Kevin Dagg further states Lieutenant Whipple, Firefighter Parr, and firefighter Fairchild, were called in next day over this event.

Captain Kevin Dagg went on to state that, "Over time, he said things he should not have. I was given an action plan to correct my behavior." Captain Dagg stated he has been sent to three classes to correct his attitude, and further stated that others have been sent away over having a negative attitude as well.

Captain Kevin Dagg stated that in the chief's Fire Officer 2 training, he was doing a scenario, and the chief berated him in front of all present. Captain Dagg states that the next day, Assistant Chief Craig Rider called him in and told him he was supposed to counsel him. Rider said Chief

Daugherty told him he was an embarrassment to the department during training. Captain Dagg stated that he put his sweatshirt on to eat lunch. He stated that the shirts have been approved to wear at night to sleep in but are not to be worn otherwise. He stated that he is a sloppy eater, and he put it on to protect his shirt.

Captain Dagg stated that Chief Daugherty told Assistant Chief Rider to tell him take it off. He thought the chief should have told him himself. Captain Dagg tried to compare this to me telling one of my police officers to do something. Police Chief John Prewer advised him that I also use the chain of command at times to relay comments.

Captain Dagg stated that Chief Daugherty puts on that he has an open-door policy. Captain Dagg stated that Chief Daugherty is defensive about everything. Dagg stated that the Pyle Goddard incident started this; that Captain Dale McKee has had to go to EAP over this event. Captain Dagg stated there are times you would like to choke Pyle Goddard, but he is a great guy, even though he is a fuck-up.

Captain Dagg stated that Pyle Goddard and Chief Daugherty don't like each other; that Pyle Goddard didn't like the chief's changes; that firefighter Richard Brice asked him what we should do, and he told him what to do. Captain Dagg stated that firefighter Richard Brice, Captain Kevin Dagg, firefighter Carl Eastman, and Captain McKee met at Richard Brice's house, which began the complaint process. Captain Dagg stated they talked of a no-confidence vote and that they met later at Captain Kevin Dagg's house to finalize the list to get rid of Chief Daugherty.

Therefore, it appears that Pyle Goddard and Captain Kevin Dagg, instead of being a leader and doing the right thing, opted to construct hearsay and innuendos to try to destroy Chief Daugherty's positive creditability. It was Pyle Goddard and Captain Kevin Dagg, with his accomplices, who fabricated issues, stating half-truths.

Firefighter Ronald Parr was also interviewed and had several complaints. It is noted that when Parr speaks of the chief, he clearly displays anger. Parr, after being hired by Chief Kelly Daugherty, clearly dislikes Chief Daugherty. Parr stated that the very first month on the job, he had a conflict with the chief. Parr asked for time off for bereavement for his father-in-law, and the chief had to get clearance from Frank Lynn. When it was decided that Parr could have the time off, however, Parr told Chief Kelly Daugherty, "Oh, never mind. I do not really care for my in-laws. I do not need to go to the funeral." Chief Daugherty was shocked by Parr's behavior and noted this in Parr's personnel file.

Parr made claims that Chief Daugherty has caused him not to be promoted, for which he dislikes him. Parr admits during his interview that he "personally [doesn't] like Chief Daugherty." (An additional caution regarding the interview of Ron Parr—during the interview with Tom and Mark Templeton, Tom was asked who would exaggerate about the chief or who might be out to simply get the chief during this inquiry. Tom and Mark Templeton both stated, "Ron Parr has always been one to run his mouth and over-exaggerate." He clearly does not like Chief Daugherty.)

Parr states that Captain James Pickings told him he would not make lieutenant, as the chief "had it out" for him. Captain Pickings told him that if he wanted the position, he would have to talk to the "old man." Parr said Pickings stated he would deny telling Parr about this (he would lie). Police Chief John Prewer asked Parr if he wished to file a complaint against Captain James Pickings as his supervisor stating that he would lie against him, and he stated, "No, only Chief Daugherty."

Police Chief John Prewer said, "You've got to be kidding me. You have a captain who says he will lie against you, and you don't want to file a complaint against him?"

He responded, "I'm here now." Parr still would not file a complaint against Captain James Pickings. I talked with Parr about the fact that he didn't even know if Captain Pickings was telling the truth about what the chief said, but he did not want to file a complaint against Captain Pickings—only Chief Daugherty.

This goes to my judging Parr on his complaints against the chief. Parr does not even know if Captain Pickings is telling him the truth about the chief, and Captain Pickings is saying, as his supervisor, that he will lie against one of his firefighters (Parr). Nevertheless, Parr's focus is only on the chief, and it is unknown even if the chief said this. Parr states, "I personally don't like him, but as an executive, he does an excellent job."

Police Chief John Prewer also interviewed Captain Kent Blackman. When asked about inappropriate behavior, Blackman stated that the chief has done nothing toward him. Blackman did state that he heard the chief make a rude comment about the county flight nurses. (Police Chief John Prewer was interested as to why, if it made him "feel funny" and it was an issue, he would have forgotten about the comment being made until someone hunting issues against the chief reminded him he was even there.)

Chief Kelly Daugherty was also asked about this incident and stated it was Assistant Chief Craig Rider who made the comment. Chief Daugherty corrected Assistant Chief Rider immediately when this occurred.

Police Chief Prewer asked Captain Blackman how the complaints got started and what got everyone now interested in filing a complaint against the chief. Captain Blackman was visibly nervous, not wanting to talk about his part in the chief's complaints.

Captain Blackman stated that at the beginning of this complaint process, Richard Brice and Carl Eastman approached him about what things he knew about the chief. Captain Blackman appeared to be trying purposely not to reveal something during this line of questioning.

Finally, at the end of the interview, Captain Blackman went back to this topic and stated that he wanted to make sure he answered this question. Police Chief Prewer advised Captain Blackman that he was to tell the truth about the questions asked. Captain Blackman was extremely nervous about answering and beat around the bush, finally stating that, *"It was Captain Kevin Dagg, Captain Dale McKee, Richard Brice, Eastman, and [himself] who had met to put the complaint letter together."* Captain Blackman was very hesitant about revealing this, as if trying to hide this until the last minute before he left the room. Only after being reminded that he had to tell the truth did he give this up. Captain Blackman stated the Pyle Goddard incident started the complaint against the chief. Captain Blackman was asked about non-Township personnel being allowed to do medical procedures on patients, and he advised it would *not* be generally okay to allow a non-Township person to do this.

Captain Blackman stated, "I don't know that I would call it a hostile work environment." He did state that he had an issue with the chief, in that Captain Blackman made a call on a fire engine that resulted in the engine of the vehicle blowing up, and the new motor cost the Township $25,000. Captain Blackman stated that this was a terrible incident for him. He stated that he left for vacation the next day, and he had to go to a library and send back a report on what had happened to the chief. He said he had a tough time with this event.

Police Chief Prewer reported on Captain Blackman's observations and information, which led Prewer to believe that Captain Blackman was very guarded and extremely nervous in his interview. Captain Blackman had to be asked several times about issues and had to be reminded that he was required to be truthful during the interview. Captain Blackman would answer part of the question and see if his answer would suffice. Upon probing with further questions, Chief Prewer would find there was more to the story that Captain Blackman did not initially give up. Captain Blackman acted as if he was hiding things in his interview.

I think it is also important to note that Blackman recently made a decision to drive a fire truck after it was acting up, and it blew the motor, resulting in a repair bill of $25,000. It is reported that Chief Kelly Daugherty addressed Blackman hard over this event. I note this as Blackman could have some issues left over from the chief over this event. Blackman defined this as a "terrible" incident for him. Blackman's statements and feelings toward the chief over this incident could play into his wanting to complain about the chief, to get back at him.

Lieutenant Robert Story had no issues of inappropriate behavior with Chief Kelly Daugherty but wanted to point out that he did not ask the union to bring complaints forward; they just did it. Lieutenant Story stated he felt like the union was using him.

Lieutenant Eric Brooks also stated that he had no issues of inappropriate behavior with Chief Kelly Daugherty. When asked if he had any other issues with Chief Kelly Daugherty, he stated "yes." Lieutenant Eric Brooks stated that he let his advanced-care life-support card expire through oversight. Lieutenant Timothy Brooks stated that it was found during a spot check and that he was brought to the trustees over his card being expired. Lieutenant Brooks stated that he originally was going to be hit with forty-eight hours of "no pay." He stated that he accepted the punishment, but the next day, the chief added a third day's pay to it and added the charge of insubordination because, according to the chief, he hesitated when he answered questions. Lieutenant Brooks blames Chief Kelly Daugherty for his inactions and not covering up for his mistakes.

According to the trustees' records, the "story" that Lieutenant Eric Brooks tells is found to be false. The trustees imposed all of the three-day suspension, and Chief Kelly Daugherty had nothing to do with their decision. This decision was made with the advice of Lawrence Gray, the Packer Township labor attorney. Lieutenant Eric Brooks went on to state further that they were lied to regarding the wellness program. Lieutenant Brooks stated that the chief violated the Health Insurance

Portability and Accountability Act by being allowed to find out personal information about them. Lieutenant Brooks stated that the chief would call people in and talk with them about their medical issues.

The facts clearly show that Chief Kelly Daugherty had permission from the trustees, Administrator Peter Graywater, and the Township attorney, to discuss the medical findings of each of the firefighters and with the assistance of Dr. Bradley Moore, the Fire Protection District's medical director, and developed an action plan to help the employee.

Lieutenant Brooks stated that the Pyle Goddard event was what started this. He stated that this was a workable call. Lieutenant Brooks also stated that 99 percent of patients in this state are not going to be saved. He stated that they didn't have the first round of drugs in, and Ron Parr didn't get a good IV. Lieutenant Brooks stated that he knows of no rule that would not allow Pyle Goddard to help.

Lieutenant Eric Brooks' older brother is Timothy Brooks. Timothy Brooks was also interviewed by Police Chief John Prewer and had no new complaints on Chief Daugherty. Timothy Brooks did state that after the 2001 situation, "My career was put on definite slow track."

Timothy Brooks stated that Chief Kelly Daugherty "did nothing illegal, just made my life rough." Timothy Brooks would not bring up new ideas "because it would be shot down." Police Chief Prewer asked when had he been shot down; he responded *at the career meetings.* Timothy Brooks said he talked with Peter Graywater about the chief abusing overtime and felt Administrator Graywater would not listen to him. Peter Graywater was the one to impose the overtime instead of hiring additional firefighters, as the chief requested.

Timothy Brooks stated that the Goddard's were allowed to work together and the Brooks family was not. Timothy Brooks then turned around and said, "Sometimes we would work together, and sometimes we could not." Brooks said, "Chief Kelly Daugherty said we couldn't work together."

Police Chief Prewer asked, "Don't you think the chief has an obligation to protect a family? What if something tragic happened, and he had two family members working the same thing and both were killed? Don't you think a chief has to think about these issues?" (Prewer observed that it was quite clear this type of thought never entered Timothy Brooks' mind. It was all about Timothy Brooks blaming Chief Kelly Daugherty for Brooks' inadequacies.) Police Chief John Prewer then said, "Mr. Timothy Brooks, your son works here, and this is all about you wanting to work with your son, isn't it? Don't you think it would be bad if the chief had both of you on the same thing and you both were killed? Don't you think that's an issue? Have you ever file a grievance?"

Brooks responded, "I threatened to file a grievance but never did."

Prewer then asked Brooks, "So you blame the chief for your career hitting the skids and you not advancing you career. Let me ask you this: have you ever taken a promotional test?"

Brooks responded, "No, it would be a waste of time."

Prewer asked, "How can you blame the chief for your career and not even take the test to start with? If you do not take the test, how can you not blame yourself for not advancing your career? Convenient to blame the chief, if you don't even take the test. Let me ask you this: why do you keep blaming the chief for all your problems and he is holding you down?

"It is obvious that if Chief Kelly did not like Timothy Brooks, then why would he hire your son after the 2001 incident? Why would he hire and promote your brother after the 2001 incident? Why would he hire your nephew?" Prewer further said, "If I didn't like a guy like you are portraying, then why would I bring on more Timothy Brook's to outnumber me?"

Brooks stated, "Yeah, I wondered about that myself." He admitted the firefighters have been talking among themselves about their interview with Chief Prewer. This would be in violation of agreement they signed with Chief Prewer.

Brooks had been getting increasingly angry with Chief Prewer during the interview. He blurted out, "You're hearing what you want to hear." He said, "We don't trust the trustees because of his relationship with them." Timothy Brooks brought up something about a raise that occurred some time ago. It was Brooks who agreed to the five-cent raise—not Chief Kelly Daugherty. Brooks stated, "As much as I dislike him, he is an intelligent man."

Brooks remained very angry and confrontational throughout most of the interview, and again, at the end of the interview, he stated, "You are hearing what you want to hear!" Brooks clearly dislikes Chief Kelly Daugherty. This can be clearly drawn from his own admissions. This appears to have been going on for years and certainly prior to him filing complaints against Chief Daugherty in 2001. There have been several interviews from fire personnel from the 2001 era that claim people had agendas against the chief. Timothy Brooks is one of those people.

Police Chief John Prewer did question Timothy Brooks' blaming the chief for everything wrong in his career, especially when he didn't take the on the responsibility to even take a promotional test or do other things to advance himself. Police Chief Prewer noted that when he would bring up things that pointed out to him his responsibility to step up to the plate in his own career, Prewer would be blamed of "hearing what I want to hear." Chief Prewer stated that he believed Timothy Brooks' interview to be suspect in value in this inquiry due to this. Brooks blames Chief Kelly Daugherty, the trustees, and Police Chief John Prewer, but takes no responsibility toward himself.

Patrick Johnson was hired shortly after David Burke left, as the new training and safety officer. Chief Prewer also interviewed Patrick Johnson, who stated that he has never seen the chief be inappropriate at any time. Patrick Johnson did express his opinion on operational issues, however, he has not addressed them to the chief—the person he needs to address his opinions to.

Instead, Patrick Johnson used this meeting to vent his frustrations. Patrick Johnson also joined the bandwagon and has failed to perform his job properly. Police Chief John Prewer later told me, Chief Daugherty, which Captain Jackson is constantly whining and complaining.

Chief Prewer also interviewed the secretary of the Packer Township Professional Firefighters Union, Carl Eastman. Prewer noted that Eastman would not look at the chief when addressing his concerns but instead would look down. This might be a sign that Carl Eastman is reading from a script and being deceptive.

Eastman expressed hearsay issues and said he was present when Chief Kelly Daugherty addressed the county hospital nurse situation. Chief Daugherty stated that Craig Rider stated these words, not him. Eastman indicated that he was upset about the Packer Township Fire Protection District wellness program and said that the chief said, "He owns them." This statement was later confirmed by the Packer Township labor attorney that Chief Kelly Daugherty stated that the Township owns the medical records—not the individuals. It is interesting on how the union personnel would twist the words to their benefit.

Chief Prewer began questioning Carl Eastman about the failure of the supervisors at the fire department to do their jobs. Prewer stated, "You guys list supervisors as some of your complainants and witnesses to complaints." Prewer advised that most of the supervisors had failed to do their jobs in reporting over the six-year span what they had seen and heard. He said, "If this is just not about one person, then you should want to file a complaint on all the supervisors for not doing their job. They failed time and time again to report the things that they say they saw that they believed to be complaints."

Prewer said, "If these complaints are not about just going after one person, then you should want to file complaints against the supervisors who failed to do their jobs. Let's get Richard Brice, union president, on the phone and get him down here and let's clean out all the supervisors who failed to do their job. Surely, if this is not just about one person, then you should, on behalf of all firefighters that were done wrong, file a complaint on all the supervisors now."

Prewer then said, "Let's go ahead get Brice down here and let's file the complaint." Chief Prewer told him, "One of the firefighters had pointed at me and told me that I owed him a safe place to work. Carl Eastman, you and Brice owe them a safe place to work, so let's clean house now while we are looking at it; let's file the complaint."

Carl Eastman stated, *"I'm not going to do that."*

Chief Prewer said, "I don't understand. Let us get rid of all the bad supervisors now. Let's file the complaint."

Eastman stated again that he did not want to file on the other supervisors. I said, "Carl Eastman, you're making me think this is just about one person, Chief Kelly Daugherty; this isn't really about just making the fire department better, is it?" Carl Eastman again stated he was not going to file a complaint against the other supervisors.

Chief Prewer said, "Carl Eastman, I'm starting to think this is just about going after one guy. Why aren't we addressing the other supervisors?" Carl Eastman stated that the supervisors are victims in his eyes. Prewer said, "We pay these guys to do their jobs, and if they are not doing their jobs, how is that being a victim? Let's file the complaint," and he refused.

Chief Prewer finished with, "You're making me think this is just about one guy."

Prewer observed that during this line of questioning, Carl Eastman was sweating down the sides of his face and refused to look at me other than a couple of glances. He stated that people hate their jobs. As we continued this line of discussion, Carl Eastman barked out, "These are crimes—sexual harassment."

Prewer said, "Crimes—sexual harassment? Well, I'm a policeman. I deal with crimes. Tell me what the crimes are, Carl Eastman." Eastman then became frustrated and backed off the "crimes" comment, and stated they are sexual harassment.

Prewer said, "Wait a minute. When Richard Brice was here, he was very cautious to not say sexual harassment."

Eastman said, "We have made no claims of sexual harassment; we didn't do that, did we?"

Prewer said, "Your union president stated there are no claims at this time of sexual harassment. Did I miss something?"

Eastman then backed off the claim of sexual harassment. Prewer said, "Carl Eastman, it didn't escape me that your union president and your three-page complaint was very cautious to not use the words *sexual harassment*. I noticed in your 2001 complaint against the chief there was a claim of sexual harassment. However, the chief was only found to have violated improper touching and inappropriate behavior."

Prewer said, "It hasn't escaped me that this time around, you guys used the same terms of improper touching and inappropriate behavior, as if to try and make sure it fit within what appears to be your theme of continuing pattern. It looks as if you used these terms against the chief on purpose, to try to make this a continuing pattern. *Am I off base with my thoughts that you guys specifically used these words to try to make this a continuing pattern?*"

Eastman stated, "I can't say it didn't give us the idea."

Prewer said, "As the union VP, show me this isn't just about one guy, when so many have done wrong. Let's go ahead and file a complaint on all the supervisors at this time and clean this whole thing up."

He responded, "We don't want to file anything on any other supervisors."

Prewer said, "Okay, Carl Eastman, explain to me why now? Why, when your complaint deals with six years' worth of stuff?"

Eastman stated, "It was the Pyle Goddard incident." Eastman then went back to trying to cover for the supervisors who had failed, and stated, "The supervisors are not the root of the problem."

Chief Prewer said, "They are being paid to do their job, and if they are too weak to do it, then we should get rid of them."

Eastman continued to try to make excuses for the other supervisors and why they should not be complained on. Eastman, at the end of the interview, went back and again exclaimed, "This is sexual harassment, and these are crimes!" Observations of Carl Eastman described visible sweating at various times during the interview. He very seldom made eye contact. Eastman became frustrated easily and would blurt things out; he was nervous throughout the interview.

Chief Prewer purposely used this confrontational line of questioning to see how Carl Eastman would react. It is clear by his interview that the union is strictly after only one person. It is clear that they will not pursue and are refusing to pursue other supervisors who have failed to perform their jobs.

Carl Eastman confirms that the Pyle Goddard event started this whole issue. He confirms that the individuals who drafted the complaint looked at the 2001 complaint and purposely drafted this complaint to try to bolster the argument of "continuing pattern," as has been stated as one of the reasons the chief should be fired. *Carl Eastman confirmed that after the Pyle Goddard event, they went "shopping" to find everything wrong with the chief that they could come up with.*

Assistant Chief Craig Rider, in an interview with Police Chief John Prewer, stated that he has no issues with Chief Kelly Daugherty relating to touching or inappropriate behavior. Craig Rider stated, "He has not seen or been made aware of any of these type of issues since he has been employed here. He stated that no employee has brought any such complaint to his attention." Craig Rider further stated that operationally, the chief is an excellent, "brilliant" inside chief and excellent politician. He stated he is a very honest and intelligent man.

District Chief Michael Baum also spoke with Chief Prewer. Baum stated he believed 99 percent of the 2001 complaint was just people stirring the pot, and they had an agenda. Baum was part of that group, but has since recanted. Baum stated the chief is dedicated to department and township.

As far as the Pyle Goddard incident, District Chief Michael Baum stated that Pyle Goddard picked at the chief for years. He stated that he warned Goddard to stop, but Goddard would not. He stated that Pyle Goddard screwed up pretty seriously, so he resigned. Baum stated that firefighters in the past were fed up with Pyle Goddard.

Captain Dale McKee had been with the department since May 2000 and provided comments to Chief John Prewer. McKee stated, "I have a good working relationship with Chief, and we do joke back and forth with each other." Captain Dale McKee stated that Assistant Chief Huston gave him a frown and walked away one day when the chief allegedly touched Captain Dale McKee. He stated he did not make this an issue, as he was afraid of intimidation.

Captain Dale McKee stated, "You feel intimidated, as he has multiple ways that he is your boss. He holds your job ransom."

Chief Prewer said, "Give me an example of demonstrated intimidation that you have seen." McKee could not give one example of demonstrated intimidation that he had witnessed.

Captain McKee stated that Chief has made multiple comments about McKee's wife's ethnic background. We have joked about her being Mexican, but sometimes it goes too far. He said something about joking about her being an aggressive Mexican running the house. Chief Prewer said, "Give me examples of where it went too far," but then he could give no example.

McKee stated it was funny, but then he kept going. Chief Prewer asked, "Did you ever say anything?"

He replied, "No." Captain Dale McKee admitted to Police Chief John Prewer that he, Pyle Captain, Captain Kevin Dagg, and others put a letter together and did not sign the complaint.

One of the part-time firefighters was the son of Timothy Brooks. Anthony Brooks, stated to Chief Prewer that he had never had a personal incident with the chief. Anthony Brooks did state that even if it is snowing or sleeting outside, the chief makes you wash the fire equipment. Brooks stated that they are restricted to their stations and not allowed to leave, even to run errands. We have to bring our food in ahead of time. Anthony Brooks stated that it is an abuse of power by the chief that they cannot go out in a pumper to go through a drive-thru to pick up food. Brooks stated that the public needs to see us out … that is good.

Prewer said, "What do you think the public thinks when they see a $500,000 pumper burning $4-plus diesel fuel at the Taco Bell drive-thru when you go to get your taco? What happens when someone blows a stop sign and hits the $500,000 pumper, and we no longer have that to use on the next fire? How do you think the public will feel about that?"

Anthony Brooks' response was that is an abuse of power by the chief because all the other departments get to take their trucks out. *Prewer said, "You really want to make this a complaint that you can't drive a $500,000 pumper through Taco Bell?"*

Anthony Brooks stated, "Yes."

Brooks further complained that he was ordered in at times, thus increasing minimum staffing made us thin at times. Chief Prewer said, "You mean the chief increased minimum staffing to make sure you had enough people at a firehouse to be safe and do your job, and you are upset?"

He said, "Yes, he should hire more people; this makes us have to work more."

Prewer said, "So you want to file a complaint that the chief gave you more people to make sure you are safe and you are complaining?"

Anthony Brooks' response, again, was "Yes."

Prewer said, "So you don't want overtime?" He stated he did. Prewer said, "So you only want the overtime when it's convenient for you, and when you don't want it, you don't want minimum staffing?" He responded, "Yes." Timothy Brooks stated that everything is Chief Kelly Daugherty's fault.

"Everyone is entitled to be stupid, but some abuse the privilege."
—Dominique Jones

One of the part-time firefighters interviewed was Tom Templeton, who stated that there has never been an incident of this nature toward him, nor has he witnessed any event of this nature toward anyone else. Templeton stated that he has spent a fair amount of time around the chief and has not seen this. He stated that he has never seen him yelling or anything like that. Chief Prewer asked if he ever saw the chief out of line, and he stated, "I never have."

Prewer asked, "If anyone would be lying on the chief or had an axe to grind, who would it be?"

Templeton stated, "Ron Parr has always been one to run his mouth and over-exaggerates things."

I commented, "So he doesn't like the chief, and I should watch his comment," and Tom Templeton concurred.

Chief Prewer tried to contact past Captain Michael Clinton. Prewer stated that he had left a note on Mr. Clinton's door at his residence to call me, should he feel he had information pertinent to the current inquiry of complaints against Chief Kelly Daugherty. Mr. Clinton has spoken at trustees meetings and on TV about the complaints.

Once Chief Prewer was able to meet with Clinton, Prewer advised Mr. Clinton he had the floor to make any comments he desired. He began with, "I only know the 2001 stuff." John Prewer told him that he had seen him making comments about the case, and he stated that the press was hounding him to give interviews.

Clinton stated he was surprised to see the TV station show up the night he spoke at the trustees meeting. He stated he knew nothing about the current inquiry other than what he heard on TV. He stated he was surprised to hear it on TV and frankly was shocked that the union had "enough balls" to file a complaint, as they are a weak union. Mr. Clinton stated that he was a captain with the fire department here. He stated that he was really treated as the assistant chief. He stated when the last chief left (one prior to Chief Kelly Daugherty), the chief's job was offered to him. He stated that he turned it down, adding, "As a chief, you have to wear two hats, being operational and political." He stated that he was not good at the political, so he chose to stay as the "number two" guy.

Clinton stated that he was told to do the backgrounds on the fire chief candidates and that he did Chief Kelly Daugherty's background. He stated that he told the trustees not to hire Chief Kelly Daugherty. I asked him why, and he stated that he really did not have anything but a "gut feeling" but that he did not want Chief Daugherty hired. He stated when the trustees hired Chief Daugherty, he and Chief Daugherty got off to a bad start right away. Clinton claims that the trustees gave his background to Chief Daugherty and that when Chief Daugherty saw this, he got mad at Clinton. He stated that he was accused by Mr. Peter Graywater of resisting change and admitted that he indeed had resisted change by Chief Kelly Daugherty.

He claims that he had one-on-one meetings in Chief Daugherty's office that no one should have to go through. I asked him if he had made complaints, and he stated, "No." He stated Chief Daugherty has two sides to him, one that is good, and a mean side that the trustees don't see. He made the comment that, "I lost the greatest job in the world because I couldn't handle the environment."

By Clinton's own admission, part of his environment problem was resisting the changes by a new chief. He stated when Chief Daugherty came in, he drew the "war" lines. He had everyone written up for everything. He stated that he or I could both go to the firehouse and engage in horseplay, and it would probably be accepted without problem, but since Chief Daugherty drew the war lines, he cannot. Chief Prewer said, "Even if some of the stuff was horseplay, the chief can't do that?"

He responded, "No, he drew the war lines. He cannot do it." Clinton admitted that Administrator Peter Graywater has engaged in horseplay of this type while employed here. Mr. Clinton wanted to use some of the same arguments presented by some of the union members that they were afraid to say anything because they could not get a job anywhere if they did.

Prewer said, "I have trouble with that argument, as everyone, including you, Mr. Clinton, has said everyone, all the surrounding agencies, know about Chief Kelly Daugherty.

Chief Prewer explained, "If everyone knows Chief Kelly Daugherty is so terrible, and then I find fault that all these other agencies would hold that against you." The other argument is that if we told, nothing would be done.

Chief Prewer pointed out to Mr. Clinton that he was saying the same. He then explained to Mr. Clinton that he himself proved that wrong, in that he filed the 2001 complaint, it was investigated, and the chief was disciplined, so that argument does not wash either. Prewer said, "You come in and blame the trustees and everyone for letting it continue, when the trustees didn't know any of these complaints, as the firemen didn't make them."

I asked, "How can you blame them for letting things continue when no one has complained?" I said, "You say 'do the right thing,' but really that means do what you want … you personally were not happy with the 2001 outcome."

Prewer asked, "What is the right thing? Is it what you [Clinton] want? Well, what if that is not what other people say is the right thing, who is right?" Clinton blamed the chief for Mr. Goddard leaving. He told a long story about how Goddard would run from his house next to the firehouse to staff the equipment when a call came in. He stated Chief Daugherty told me to reprimand him for the policy violation of running at a call. He stated that Goddard then started walking fast to the station and Chief Daugherty wanted him reprimanded.

I said, "So Goddard is running and picking at the chief, so the chief does something about that, and instead of stopping the behavior, Goddard now runs fast just to jab the chief, and you want to blame this all on the chief?"

He stated, "Chief Daugherty wanted you written up for stupid little things." I pointed out, "Jabbing the chief is not stupid also?" I told him as a chief, I would get tired of that.

Clinton clearly does not like Chief Kelly Daugherty on a personal level. He admits that he resisted change to the department and didn't like the fact that Chief Daugherty was hired. He clearly blames Chief Daugherty for "losing the greatest job in the world," because he couldn't handle the environment; but clearly it is an environment he helped create in his resisting change. It is clear that Clinton made problems with Chief Kelly Daugherty from the beginning.

Clinton stated that all recommendations by prior departments of Chief Kelly Daugherty were good, but he had a "gut feeling," with nothing else supporting that, and actually saying the opposite, that Chief Kelly Daugherty should not have been hired. Mr. Clinton stated that he has no idea of what the current complaints are against Chief Kelly Daugherty, other than what he heard on TV, but he insists that Chief Kelly Daugherty should be fired.

Chief Prewer stated that he cannot determine Chief Kelly Daugherty's involvement in their personality clash, as it was too long ago and surely involves many dynamics but due to the personal dislike of Chief Kelly Daugherty that Mr. Clinton exhibits. As the investigator, *Police Chief Prewer finds it hard to give any credible weight to Clinton's comments.* Mr. Clinton clearly wants to have Chief Kelly Daugherty fired. It is impossible to determine if that is for his own personal reasons, for what he appears to want me, Chief Prewer to think—he simply wants to save the fire department.

I find it hard to believe and too coincidental to believe his story that he knows nothing of how the press received this information, as it is very coincidental that the news crews only showed up at a trustees meeting the night Mr. Clinton came to speak and haven't been back since. In the end, Mr. Clinton, by his own words, stated he knows nothing about what is going on now but appears to want a forum to involve himself, using a trustees meeting to blame people; coincidence that the press is there to televise it, desiring interview time with me, all about something he claims he knows nothing about.

Even though Mr. Clinton may appear truthful in some of his claims, his comments must be treated as suspect, and I believe this all goes to the credibility of Mr. Clinton as a usable witness in this investigation.

> *"Creditability is like virginity; once you lose*
> *it, you can never get it back"*
> —*Citron Reports*

Captain James Pickings also spoke with Police Chief John Prewer, who asked, "What was the demeanor of the firehouse, and what is the behavior?"

Captain Pickings stated, "There is, on a daily level, jokes, horseplay, with the firefighters." Prewer then asked if any of their comments ever reached the level of a sexual overtone, and he stated that it does Pickings further stated that he has had no issue about the chief since 2001.

John Kaiser, a career firefighter who was previously targeted by Captain Blackman, Captain Kevin Dagg, and McKee as being a screw-up, told Chief Prewer that Chief Kelly Daugherty shook his hand, and the chief's finger touched his wrist. John Kaiser said this made him feel uncomfortable.

Chief Prewer asked him to explain further why he thought he was a target. Kaiser stated that Captain Jackson took him in a closed-door office and told him that he was a target of the chief. Prewer asked him when Captain Jackson told him he was a target, and he stated it was in July or August. Prewer said, "So when he touched your shoulder on the couch, you felt funny about the chief doing this, because you knew you were a target?"

He replied, "Yes."

Prewer said, "Explain this to me. You are basing your being uncomfortable when the chief touched your shoulders on the fact that you thought you were a target?"

He said, "Yes."

Prewer then stated, "You just told me you did not find out about the fact that you were supposedly the chief's target until July or August. How, then, can you base your complaint on something you didn't know, because you didn't find out about it until two years later?"

John Kaiser then looked at me and said, "Can we forget about this? Can we just scratch this off"?

Chief Prewer said, "You don't want to make this a complaint now?"

He said, "No ... can we just forget about this?"

Prewer advised him that this had already become part of the record and then asked him what the chief had done to make him feel like a target.

Kaiser stated that he had gotten some petty write-ups last year on an EMS call for going the wrong way while en route to a call. He stated that Captain McKee wanted to give him a verbal, but the chief wanted it to be a written. Chief Prewer asked him how it was found that he went the wrong way, and he stated that the previous police chief at that time started it by making it a complaint. Chief Prewer said, "So the police chief started it, and Captain McKee and the police chief relayed it to Chief Kelly Daugherty, but you do not want to file a complaint against them, just Chief Kelly Daugherty?"

He replied, "Yes."

Prewer then asked him if he had indeed gone the wrong way, and he stated that he had gone a different way than he had been told to. Prewer said, "So let me understand this again: Chief Kelly Daugherty was not present?"

His response was, "No."

"Chief Kelly Daugherty was disciplining you on what the police chief and Captain McKee told him, but you have no complaint against them?"

His response was, "No."

Prewer then asked why he would not complain against them, and he stated this was all about the chief making him a target. Chief Prewer then asked him what other write-ups he had, and he stated, "You mean now or all of them?"

He stated that he was also mad at the chief because he made him go to EAP. He stated, "I didn't need to go to EAP.'" I asked him what had happened, and he stated that he was on a non-breathing patient and "He [the chief] claims I lost composure on the call, and I got a written for losing my composure and a written for delayed response, and I don't agree with this."

Chief Prewer asked if the chief was present on the call, and he stated he was not. I said, "So the ranking officers on the scene told Chief Kelly Daugherty that you lost your composure, and you got a couple of write-ups for this call?"

He stated, "Yes."

Chief Prewer said, "Then you must want to file a complaint against these officers as well as Chief Kelly Daugherty?"

He stated, "No, just Chief Kelly Daugherty."

Prewer said, "You stated you didn't think this was appropriate, and you're mad you had to go to EAP. Why would you not file a complaint against the fire commanders?" Prewer pointed out to him that if the chief was not on the scene, then he was going off what the commanders told him in order to recommend discipline. Why would he not be mad at them? Because if he didn't do this, then these commanders lied to the chief. Prewer asked, "Do you want to file a complaint on the commanders present for giving the chief the bad info or not?"

John Kaiser then stated, "Just mark this off."

Chief Prewer then asked John Kaiser if the chief had ever created a hostile work environment, and John Kaiser said, "Not that I know of."

Prewer asked John Kaiser, "Other than the captain telling you that you were a target, do you have anything else?"

John Kaiser stated, "No."

Chief Prewer then asked, "Did the chief ever tell you that you were a target?" and he said no.

CHAPTER 10
Unethical Organizational Behavior

*"If you think you might be able to get
away with doing it, don't do it."*
—*Texas Senator Carl Parker*

Are ethical foundations in America's fire service eroding? I find it interesting that during my research, I found that what's ethical to one person might not be ethical to another.

However, from a leadership perspective, it is about determining what other people expect of us. Our citizens and supervisors expect us to be open, to communicate with one another, and to be honest. You would think that this principle would be easy—but I found differently. The main point of addressing ethical behavior is not necessarily to define it but to get people thinking about it—being reflective and introspective about what it means to them and how they can exhibit good behavior.

The fire service as a whole needs to be concerned with the type of reputation and management issues addressed in Cumberland Valley white paper. Such incidents involving firefighters and the fire service are occurring nationwide and frequently strike a common chord. The frequency with which these incidents are reported appears to be increasing, and collectively they are liable to cause great harm.

For better or worse, there is an ample supply of events to study and from which to draw lessons to learn. A review of the root causes of hundreds of ethical lapses involving members of the fire service in recent years yields a critical, if not surprising, finding. Just as many fire service operations-related failures have been attributed to leadership breakdowns; the same goes for these social, cultural, and ethical lapses.

Leaders need to understand that this is more than pen to paper. Codes of ethics and rules of conduct are of no use if they are not lived every day and used to hold people accountable, even when it is unpopular. That takes courage, and that deserves our support.

It would appear, especially in this situation that a number of firefighters feel that they automatically have a sense of entitlement, just because they are firefighters. If the result of a "hero" status within the fire service is not properly balanced with a sense of ethical responsibility, then some fire service leaders fear that individual firefighters can develop a harmful attitude of entitlement that creates an expectation of double standards.

This then can create an expectation that one standard of behavior for the public but tolerates a different standard that exists for "hero" firefighters. While unselfish service as a firefighter deserves to be honored, a false sense of special entitlement with different rules must not be allowed to flourish.

According to the International Association of Fire Chiefs "Fire Chief under Attack" article, managers who may also be union members are placed in an extremely difficult position, because it is impossible to be loyal to both the union and management when the union is attacking the fire chief.

Union action has been taken against certain union members simply because they conscientiously performed their assigned duties and refused to cooperate with plans to undermine the fire chief. This is all in an attempt to gain control of the township fire service—period.

The IAFC is considered the professional organization representing fire chiefs, but it has previously never become directly involved in defending its members. Its primary missions are to enhance the ability of its individual members to carry out their duties and to improve public safety. It has never tried to enhance the personal awards that are available to its members or to represent their interest on their political turf. Indeed, the IAFC has stayed away from conflict situations, not wanting to judge the performance of individual members and potentially find fault with their actions or policies.

The budget and staff resources of the IAFF, compared to the IAFC, are overwhelming. IAFC publications seldom report on individual conflict situations and have not provided significant insight on the subject. Recognizing this apparent weakness, the IAFF has successfully isolated individual chiefs, positioning them as one individual under attack from a large national organization.

One of the commonly used tactics is the vote of no confidence. In the majority of cases, this has been directed toward chiefs who have been appointed from outside the department or chiefs who have held office for a relatively short time. The vote of no confidence is a direct challenge to the authority of the chief and is intended to force the chief to resign, to be dismissed, or to retreat on controversial issues. It also has the secondary effect of severely demoralizing the other members of the fire department management team.

A second tactic is to overload the system with grievances. While a grievance procedure is designed to resolve issues, it is easy to abuse the system by filing numerous official grievances over trivial issues and refusing to settle on any of them. In some cases, as many as one hundred grievances have been filed at one time. This tactic is intended to make the fire chief appear as an unreasonable person, incapable of functioning in a normal labor-management process. It is also intended to take up so much of management's time that progress is stopped and frustration is instilled.

The battle for credibility is one of the more important tactical activities—specifically, the fire chief's activities. The fire chief's opponents will use union publications, meetings, the public news media, and the rumor mill to spread misinformation about policies and decisions, warning the members of dire consequences to their personal welfare and warning the public of reductions in public protection that will result from the chief's policies.

The fire chief can counter those statements with factual information, but the battle for credibility often determines which story will be accepted. This battle often extends to character assassination when accusations are made about the individual's personal objectives, behavior, finances, living arrangements, sexual behavior, health, and similar topics.

In at least four cases, the delegates gathered at an IAFF annual convention have adopted a "motion of censure" against the individual fire chief. This is considered the form of ultimate disapproval of the individual on behalf of the entire IAFF. Typically, one of the locals presents the motion, and only statements in support of the motion are heard. The chiefs were not informed that such action was pending nor given an opportunity to respond to the accusations.

The most irresponsible act of personalizing an issue has been to accuse a fire chief of personal responsibility for the injury or death of a firefighter. In a recent case, the contents of a National Institute for Occupational Safety and Health investigative report were deliberately and incorrectly represented to insinuate that the fire chief was responsible for the death of a firefighter. It appears that the IAFF was directly involved at the national level in planning and manipulating this situation because of an ongoing local dispute with the chief. As with the motions of censure, the IAFF issued press releases to the local media and used its own publications, attempting to damage the chief's reputation.

The Packer Township Trustees (Neil, Lowe, and Bode), along with the administrator, Peter Graywater, are guilty of allowing the firefighter to freely access and circumvent the elected officials' mandate. In turn, these elected and appointed officials have lowered their standards and gave into hearsay and innuendo. According to Chief Prewer's findings, Chief Kelly Daugherty did nothing wrong; however, he became the political football for doing his job and the right thing.

Peter Graywater and Frank Lynn have often asked if I was interested in running for elected office. It now appears that I had placed the township in a "good light" over the past decade, that I may have been a threat to the current elected officials. Whatever happened to doing the job right and not worrying about how to position yourself with the elected officials?

Packer Township Administrator Peter Graywater and his assistant, Frank Lynn, have been in office for quite a long time. However, the way they both treated me—a person who has exceeded their expectations for over eleven years—is unspeakable. In fact, Dr. Anthony Romano stated these same words.

When I first came to Packer Township, the township attorney, Lawrence Gray, provided me some advice and a pecking order on how Peter Graywater and Frank Lynn behave toward department heads. He stated that *they* come first, then the firefighters, then the citizens, ending with the elected officials.

Lawrence Gray said, *"In order to survive, you need to follow this order."* I could see in Gray's body language that even he realized that this was not an appropriate method by which to conduct business and to treat people—but Lawrence Gray is an attorney, looking for billable hours.

My ability to work an operating budget and to stay fiscally sound was quite impressive. *When I would ask Peter Graywater about having* the Fire Protection District receive the interest on the fire levy money, *Graywater would tell me to shut up and don't worry about it.* The last time I asked Graywater about keeping his promise and allowing the Fire Protection District to receive the interest money, *he slammed his foot against his desk and yelled at me not to talk about that interest money ever again. Peter Graywater acted as if this was his money, not the hardworking taxpayers'.*

During Halloween time, Frank Lynn would have me collect money from the other department heads and Fire Protection District officers and firefighters to help purchase candy for the Rotary Club. Lynn would often tell me, *"You need to pay to play."* His meaning led me to ask what he was talking about. *Frank Lynn stated that in order to keep your job, you need to help pay for Halloween candy, chip in for our elected official campaigns, and anything else that comes our way. I was quite disappointed in Frank Lynn's behavior.*

When I reached my time in grade with the pension board, I elected to enter the retirement option program. This program allowed eligible police officers and firefighters to continue to work; however, it allowed the remaining eight years of working to be placed in an annuity.

This annuity profited both the pension system and the fire/police officer seeking this benefit. There was no additional obligation or resources needed from the employer. However, when I told Frank Lynn that I had entered this voluntary program, he stated, *"Well, it is like you are already retired."*

These inappropriate words are an example of how Frank Lynn treats people. He knows that I am still a young man and have brought a huge amount of good to the township, but since he is in the Employees' Retirement System, which does not have the retirement annuity benefit, he feels that he has to stab me, and in his mind (my opinion) to get back at me.

One Saturday morning, trustee Arthur Bode come to my home, with his mother still in his truck, and asked if I would deliver his and the mayor's re-election pamphlets throughout our neighborhood. He looked at me like I had better not say no or there would be hell to pay.

When we passed the fire levy, one of the pieces of apparatus we were to purchase was a hundred-foot ladder truck. After following the state law on purchases in excess of $25,000, we were able to purchase the ladder truck, with the Richmond County prosecutor's approval. This new apparatus definitely fits our township's need; however, I later found out, by asking Peter Graywater specifically, that he received two tickets to the Indianapolis Motor Speedway—the Indy 500—from the fire apparatus vendor.

Graywater did tell Chief Daugherty that he went to the event, with tickets worth $400 each. From a legal perspective, Peter Graywater violated the ethics law in accepting these tickets, and nothing has ever been done about this.

> *"Honesty stands at the gate and knocks, and bribery enters in"*
> *—Barnabe Rich*

After my first year of employment with Packer Township, Frank Lynn told me, while we were at a local restaurant one evening, that I just lost four weeks of vacation. I was amazed to find out that he (in my opinion) purposely had me lose this vacation time to see how I would react. As time progressed, I lost additional accrued vacation time, in part that I took my position seriously and stayed back in the Fire Protection District to ensure coverage.

Is this how you want your appointed and political leaders to conduct themselves? Does the term "trustees" really fit this organization? I really find it disgusting that the Packer Township firefighters actually defend cheaters and liars by stating, as Richard Brice has, "Everyone knows what goes on in a firehouse—everyone cheats, lies, and steals."

As a fire chief who took a once-small, splintered, unorganized group of misfits and acted as a change agent to form the flagship of emergency services in Richmond County, my heart has always been in the right place, and I have the right to call out the firefighters on their behaviors. I am disgusted and appalled by the behavior of these firefighters. Firefighting is a noble profession; however, the Packer Township firefighters have now placed it at an all-time low.

Police Chief John Prewer stated it best during the course of his investigation when he stated, "One of the issues I knew I would face would be the laundry list of every person's personal gripes about how the chief does business. I have attached a list of some of the petty and ridiculous complaints that were listed as an abuse of power by the chief."

I am not trying to belittle that person's individual complaint as much as make a point. By the mere nature of the position, the fire chief has power. It is his responsibility to lead the department; if not, eighty people will go in eighty directions. Each of these orders, no matter how trivial, may seem to an outsider as having no purpose. Fire and police personnel need to practice following orders—big and small.

At the scene of an emergency, fire and police personnel must be practiced at following orders. It is the very fabric of what saves people's lives and keeps us safe at the scene. If we do not follow orders, someone could be injured or killed. Someone has to be in charge at a scene, whether you like each of his or her calls for action or not.

There were claims like, "The chief made me wash the cars three times in a row or clean the bays over and over, or he interrupted our dinner to do work," as examples of what I heard as some "abuses of power." Those orders may simply have been just that—orders. The orders may have been the chief having a bad day or the chief overstepping his bounds some, or it may simply have been that the firefighter was just too lazy to work and has to be told to do so and now wants to complain.

In the event that a supervisor either is the subject of it himself or sees someone or hears of someone being harassed, retaliated against, etc., they have a duty by their position to report that incident for review. Supervisors are also the managers of our employees and are charged with both the well-being and safety of the personnel they command. Packer Township Police Chief John Prewer's final report clearly states:

"There was a <u>COMPLETE FAILURE</u> on the part of Captain(s) Kevin Dagg, Tracy Blackman, Dale McKee, James Pickings & Patrick Jackson; Lieutenant(s) Robert Story, Lloyd Whipple, Anthony Gibbs, Eric Brooks, Gilbert Brown, Wayne Folsom; District Chief Michael Baum & Assistant Chief Craig Rider to do their jobs."

Each of these supervisors was listed as complainants or witnesses to events claimed in the union complaint or were found to have been complainants or witnesses to events during the interviews. Each of these supervisors had an obligation as management personnel to bring forth the complaints at the time they happened, if they were indeed factual.

The other disturbing fact that I observed was that in each case where a firefighter made a complaint, if the information revealed that either a supervisor witnessed or they had told a supervisor about the incident, they did not want that supervisor disciplined for doing nothing about the complaint.

On every complaint filed, it was only Chief Kelly Daugherty they desired to see punished. It is disturbing that the union personnel do not want to hold all supervisors accountable for their actions and are only selective in whom they blame, that being Chief Kelly Daugherty.

Chief John Prewer, in his report, states that anytime you have an investigation of this magnitude, it has many layers and dynamics to it. It will not be as cut and dried as "did someone just do something right or wrong?" and that is exactly what I found as the investigation progressed.

The complaint period in question is from 2001 until 2008 in the current complaint filed by the fire department's union. Forty-one interviews were conducted in two and a half months. The complaint consisted of three pages. The original complaint was replaced with a second version provided by the union, which had names attached to the complaints. The second complaint had some additional complaints added, and Captain Kevin Dagg, in his interview, requested two additional complaints be added.

Complaint Resolution Available To Firefighters
A firefighter who is an employee of Packer Township has several different courses to take, should he or she feel have a complaint that should be addressed. They may address complaints through any of the following avenues:

1. Packer Township's employee handbook-prescribed complaint processes.
2. The General Operations Guidelines of the fire department.
3. The union's collective bargaining agreement, which allows for and permits grievances.
4. Labor/management meetings.

I have found *no* previous complaints filed since 2001 regarding any of the complaints listed and contained within the documents filed by the union against Chief Kelly Daugherty, which are the subject of this investigation.

I find no grievances filed by the union during this time that address any of the complaints listed in the document filed by the union in this matter. I do find an uncontested excerpt from one of the labor/management meetings dated February 2, 2007 listed as a bullet point that states, "*Labor has expressed how pleasant our working environment is and has expressed encouragement in our organization.*"

I have also found in those labor/management meetings listed time after time that "*Both management and labor really had no issues for this meeting.*" I find it a disturbing fact that the same union that brings forth this complaint in 2008 has stood silent since 2001 as related to these complaints.

The interviews confirmed that *not one* of the complainants listed as a subject or witness in this investigation has ever filed a complaint or wished to have a complaint filed against Chief Kelly Daugherty during this timeframe, as related to the 2008 complaints. This is a disturbing fact to me.

I have seen previous employees of the fire department go before the news cameras and address the township trustees in public meeting, casting blame upon the management of Packer Township for allowing a continuing pattern of wrongful events by Chief Kelly Daugherty.

It is quite clear that if even one member of the union or fire personnel issued no complaints during this time, no member of management could have the ability even to know that these complaints existed. I find the comments that township officials have allowed this behavior by Chief Kelly Daugherty to continue to be without merit. If none of the complainants or union members exercised his or her right to bring forth a complaint through any of the forums available to them, how could township officials know any problem existed? To blame the Township for their failure to address these issues is without merit.

Kevin Dagg states they first thought of putting together a vote of no confidence but then decided on the complaint format. *It is clear from the interviews that this group then went out and solicited any and all complaints they could find on the chief. They basically went on a shopping trip, trying to accumulate every complaint they could come up with.*

The shopping-trip theory has a problem, in that it allows for anyone with a grudge against the chief, previous discipline issues, or those just wanting an opportunity to remove the chief for their own personal promotional gain to bring forth questionable complaints. This was observed in the interview process.

There were clearly people with agendas making complaints. After compiling as many complaints as they could, Captain Kevin Dagg,

Richard Brice, Blackman, and Carl Eastman met at Captain Dagg's house to finalize the list. The complaint was then filed with the Township.

This, to me, appears very dangerous, in that this wasn't really about the stated issues in the complaint, as much as it appears to be about their desire for retribution against Chief Kelly Daugherty for their perception that Daugherty wronged one of their own, Pyle Goddard.

Chief Prewer states that he found a very disturbing pattern within the fire department. Supervisors have many roles in a fire organization. One of those roles is making sure that everyone—including themselves— follows established policies and procedures. The position, in itself, does not permit the luxury of hiding or making excuses for not following the rules.

In the event that a supervisor either is the subject of it him- or herself or sees someone or hears of someone being harassed or retaliated against, the supervisor has a duty by the position to report that incident for review. Supervisors are also the managers of our employees and are charged with both the well-being and safety of the personnel they command.

Each of these supervisors was listed as complainants or witnesses to events claimed in the union complaint or was found to have been complainants or witnesses to events during the interviews. Each of these supervisors had an obligation as management personnel to bring forth the complaints at the time they happened, if they were indeed factual. Many of the supervisors stated that they feared retaliation or their jobs, should they speak up.

This brings into question what else they would overlook or not report for alleged fear of losing their jobs. The other disturbing fact that I observed was that in each case where a firefighter made a complaint, and if the information revealed either that a supervisor witnessed or that they had told a supervisor about the incident, they did not want that supervisor disciplined for doing nothing about the complaint.

On every complaint filed, it was only Chief Kelly Daugherty that the "professionals" desired to see punished. It is disturbing that the union personnel do not want to hold all supervisors accountable for their actions and only be selective in whom they blame, Chief Daugherty.

DISTURBING ISSUES

I had mentioned earlier that I found it odd that the union complaint this time appeared to purposely be missing the words "sexual harassment." The claim was that this complaint was similar to and a continuing pattern of the 2001 complaint. During the interview with union president Richard Brice, I found it interesting that he quickly corrected me when I purposely used the words "sexual harassment" when speaking with him. He made it clear that the union was not claiming sexual harassment in the current complaint.

During the interview with union secretary Carl Eastman, he admitted that the people who put this complaint together did purposely look at the fact that the chief was not found in violation of any sexual harassment issues in 2001 and was only found at fault of inappropriate comment/behavior issues in 2001. In other words, they looked at the 2001 complaint and purposely tried to make sure each of the 2008 complaints matched 2001, so that they could claim "continuing behavior."

Dr. Roy Bohn, the Packer Township physician who mainly performs pre-employment and fitness-for-duty examinations, from the Austin City Center for Family Medicine, told me that he knew these unselfish firefighters were conspiring against all I had done for them—and even went as far as to say that, "They are an ungrateful bunch of assholes." Liars will do whatever it takes to make themselves look good and others bad. According to Dr. Gail Saltz, *Analogy of a Secret Life: The Psychology of Living a Lie:*

> *"Everybody lies. It may only be "white" lies, but everyone tells lies or "omits the truth" sometimes. We start lying at around age 4 to 5 when children gain an awareness of the use and power of language."*
>
> *"This first lying is not malicious, but rather to find out, or test, what can manipulated in a child's environment. Eventually children begin to use lying to get out of trouble or get something they want. White lies, those concocted to protect someone's feelings, are not a big deal at all. The person, however, who seems to feel, compelled to lie about both the small and large stuff has a problem. We often call these folks pathological liars, which is a description, not a diagnosis."*

The book further states that these people lie to protect themselves and to look good, gain financially or socially, and avoid punishment. Quite often, the person who has been deceived knows that this type of liar has, to a certain extent, deluded him- or herself and is therefore to be pitied somewhat. A much more troubling group is those who lie a lot and knowingly for personal gain.

These people may have a condition called antisocial personality disorder, also known as being a sociopath, and often get into scrapes with the law. Lying often gets worse with the passage of time. When you get away with a lie, it often impels you to continue your deceptions. In addition, liars often find themselves perpetrating more untruths to cover themselves.

We hold different people to different standards when it comes to telling the truth. We expect, for example, less honesty from politicians than from scientists. We have a vision of purity about those who are doing research, while we imagine that politicians will at least shade the truth about themselves in order to be elected.

Why do we dislike liars, especially sociopaths, so much? It is a matter of trust. When a person lies, they have broken a bond—an unspoken agreement to treat others as we would like to be treated. Serious deception often makes it impossible for us to trust another person again. Because the issue of trust is on the line, coming clean about the lie as soon as possible is the best way to mend fences. If the truth only comes out once it is forced, repair of trust is far less likely.

Dr. Gail Saltz also states that as a parent, the most important message you can send your children about lying is that you always want them to come clean with you. No matter how big a whopper they have told, remind them that you would always rather hear the truth, no matter how bad it is, than be deceived.

Tell them there is really nothing more sacred in your relationship than your trust of each other. Of course, all this presupposes that we have discovered an untruth—some people are so expert at deception that it often takes a long time to find out that we have been lied to.

> *"Destroy the seed of evil, or it will grow up to your ruin."*
> —*Aesop*

Once more, according to the Cumberland Valley white paper, "the fire service faces a host of issues that threaten its integrity and sterling public image. This risk is increased by the lightning speed at which information, and sometimes misinformation, is transmitted and propagated. Moreover, because of the continuing advent of technology, no longer can any issue be considered truly 'local' as even the most isolated of matters affecting the most far-flung of departments can sully the reputation of the entire fire service.

"Some of the issues discussed herein are not new. For example, various concerns about the association of the fire service with alcohol have long and notorious roots. By contrast, concerns with respect to other matters, such as misuse of information technology, are much more recent and assuredly other trends will continue to develop.

"Recognizing that the actions of a small minority of bad actors can have grievous widespread consequences, the fire service as a whole must be increasingly vigilant in policing itself. Through a combination of enhanced and improved internal controls, increased vigilance, and greater acceptance of personal responsibility perhaps including, but not limited to, abiding by a Code of Ethics, the fire service can ensure that it remains true to its roots and heritage of protecting and serving this great nation."

"When it comes to harassment complaints, the Township expects all employees to report any harassment of any employee to their supervisor immediately. In addition, the Packer Township Fire Protection District general operational guidelines approved and enforced by the Packer Township board of trustees, which the immediate supervisors are responsible for all details and activities that are assigned.

"In addition, the Fire Chief may recommend the dismissal of any Fire Protection District personnel for neglect of duty, any act of oppression or tyranny, any act of insubordination or disobedience, immoral or illegal conduct or conduct unbecoming an employee, violations of the rules including bribery, misfeasance, malfeasance, nonfeasance and any misconduct."

The Packer Township Firefighters identified had all elevated themselves, based on their behavior, to this level; however, the Packer Township board of trustees turned a blind eye and has refused to uphold their responsibilities.

We find it interesting that during deposition, Carl Eastman stated, "Our original request to Frank Lynn was to have the union split the cost of Chief Kelly Daugherty's investigation—so we had some control over his fate."

In deposition, Frank Lynn stated that he did know who the people were who lodged an anonymous complaint against Chief Kelly Daugherty, but had failed to explain this information to the chief.

In deposition, Lynn was asked how long he had been employed with Packer Township. Lynn stated it was from 1982 through 1991, and then he was recommissioned in 1993 as a certified police officer. Lynn was asked if he remembered a meeting in February with Richard Brice, Carl Eastman, and Arthur Bode. Lynn said, "Yes, I do."

Lynn was asked how that meeting came about. He stated, "Mr. Bode called me in the late afternoon, said that he received a call from Richard Brice, wanting to meet him around 6:00, and asked me to attend." At this point, Lynn stated that he had no idea what this meeting was regarding. Lynn was then asked if he thought there was anything inappropriate about having a meeting with the union representatives outside the scope of the workplace.

Lynn stated, "I thought it was inappropriate for an employee to contact a trustee to make an arrangement for that." Even though Lynn thought it was inappropriate, he went because his boss, Bode, said "he wanted me to go."

Lynn was asked what was the conversation about. He stated, "At first, we only talked about little nicey nicey talk. Then Richard Brice started to talk about an incident that happened [the Goddard incident], which was in reference to the procedures and policies and how to handle that incident." Lynn further indicated that once he realized what the conversation was about, he stopped Richard Brice and said, "That's operational, that this is not the place to do operational; you need to go through the chain of command."

Lynn then stated that once Richard Brice realized that he was not getting his way, Brice changed the conversation, stating that Chief Kelly Daugherty inappropriately touched him and others. No dates, names, or further details were given by Richard Brice to substantiate his allegations. Lynn then told Brice to reduce his complaint to writing and to forward it to him for review.

Lynn was asked if he told Richard Brice to give him something unsigned. Lynn stated, "I remember that once it was more than him that was, you know, the alleger, then we talked about making this, you know, so it's like a class complaint. I told him that I can take a complaint signed or unsigned. I'll have to investigate it, no matter which way."

Lynn further stated, "Richard Brice had hesitations on signing it, I can tell you this, because he said that Chief Daugherty was his friend.

Chief Daugherty was the one that, when he was seventeen years old, guided him to go to school to become a paramedic. He finished that, came back. Chief Daugherty gave him his job, and Chief Daugherty promoted him to the career, so he really didn't do this on his own. He was doing it for the union."

Lynn also stated that he believed the Pyle Goddard incident was the catalyst for the union to take this action against Chief Kelly Daugherty, a person who had worked hard to provide the Packer Township firefighters everything they need to perform their jobs.

Issues described here and in the IAFC "Fire Chief under Attack," and the "Fire Service Reputation Management" white paper are generally omnipresent on the fire service national stage; they are not isolated or limited to just the career or volunteer service, or the urban, suburban, or rural fire service.

Instead, these issues have been found to be present in the fire service nationwide, in all types of communities, and within all types of fire departments. The occurrence of such issues and events may evidence a lack or failure of leadership, and the damage wrought by public disclosure of these sorts of events often transcends the particular department involved. Once lost, a positive reputation is hard to regain.

CHAPTER 11
A Lawyer's Advice Is His Stock in Trade

*"If you compromise vital issues, you will always
lose friends and never appease your enemies."*
—*Arthur Schlesinger, Jr.*

To provide an example of how Peter Graywater and Lynn treated their
fire chief, I took the liberty of documenting their behaviors toward me
while I was stationed at the Packer Township Government Center. This
information was documented and provided to my attorney for future
use.

March 9
This evening, I called Peter Graywater at his residence to see if he wanted
me to go to in the office tonight and sign payroll—he said no—he said
to take the night off. Graywater told me that he did not promise anyone
anything—referring if I should go into work on Monday. I did ask and
he said yes—just like normal.

I told him that I go into the office at 08:00 a.m. and have a command
staff meeting at 08:15 a.m. then proceed to the safety meeting with the
police chief and Frank Lynn by 09:30. He then said he would meet with
me after the safety meeting.

March 10

I went to work as planned. I conducted our every Monday morning command staff meeting—all of the usual officers were present. I met with our administrative clerk and she told me that Assistant Chief Craig Rider signed the bills and payroll last Friday.

I then went to my safety meeting with Frank Lynn and John Prewer. After that meeting, Lynn told me that Graywater wanted to talk to me. I said okay. Frank Lynn asked me who my attorney was and I told him that I would disclose this information at a later time. Lynn also said that the firefighters are out to get rid of Chief Daugherty.

Peter Graywater came in the meeting room and told me I have two choices. Either take administrative leave or move my office to the government center, and, also that I am not to make any runs and only have contact with Assistant Chief Craig Rider. After he spoke, I asked if my contact could be with District Chief Michael Baum and not with Assistant Chief Craig Rider, and Graywater agreed.

Graywater thought he heard that the Richmond County Fire Chiefs Association was having a special meeting about the allegations (which is possible since the fire chief [association] president is a close friends with Thomas Vandyke (he actually hired him as a shift captain) and did not like me or Peter Graywater.

Graywater also asked me if he can do anything for me and I told him not at this time. Frank Lynn is to go with me to the fire department office and get what I needed to do my job. Graywater asked me if I had an attorney and I said yes, and we are going to do what you suggested to my wife and fight these lies.

March 10

While I was in my new office setting, Richard Graywater came in and I asked if he got with District Chief Michael Baum on our arrangement. He said District Chief Baum had some questions regarding evaluations, leave, and discipline. Graywater told him that the only thing the chief will not do is have contact with anyone else but him. Graywater then told me that I should tread very carefully, I am in a bad situation and I, as the fire chief needs to be very careful. Peter Graywater then said, *"You can play fire chief until you lose it."*

Graywater told me that the City of Throop city manager knows what is going on and that I should keep going to meetings and keep her informed on administrative issues, like I have always been. Peter

Graywater then asked how my wife is doing and if I needed anything and I said, no, not at this time. Today I received a telephone call from Lieutenant Devon Jeter of the Austin Division of Fire. Jeter called me to ask if I would resign/retire. I said why—I did nothing wrong. *Jeter says that you are making these guys do their jobs and they don't like that—you are making us look bad.* I asked, "How am I making you all look bad when you swore to your communities to do your job?" Jeter hung up the telephone.

March 11

Around 2:00 p.m., this date, Peter Graywater told me that Ely Wall (Richmond County administrator) wants to take me out to lunch. Peter Graywater also said that even if you come out perfect through this investigation, *"You will be perceived as adequate—nothing more."*

Around 4:45 p.m.—Police Chief John Prewer stopped by to let me know that he is starting to interview the union members first, then the command staff—he also said we would go from there. Police Chief Prewer then said that trustee Arthur Bode would only approve the wrapping of the new police cars—the new Dodge Chargers with the Hemi engines, only if when the wrapping comes off, so can purchase the Charger when the police are done and before it goes to auction. Police Chief John Prewer said that Trustee Arthur Bode wants a "Police Package" vehicle for himself.

Today I received a telephone call from Daniel Carlson, the fire chief of Middleton FD, and Brian Sweeney of the YMCA. They let me know that they know me, support me, and that I have always done the right thing. I also received a call from one of our rescue tool venders, Mr. Greg O' Conner. Greg stated in his telephone call that he admired the fact that I was insistent that training and education be the forefront for the Packer Township Firefighters, and that, "You did nothing wrong. The firefighters only want to sit around and you want them to be accountable."

March 12

Today, Cheryl Graywater (Peter Graywater's then-wife) called me to let me know that she supports me. That afternoon, Frank Lynn told me that he thought that the township could control past employees and that Pyle Goddard called Peter Graywater to let him know that he was going to attend the trustees meeting. Frank Lynn also said, *"He cannot believe these people."* Yet he allowed this circus to continue.

Peter Graywater stopped by my office this afternoon and we were talking about healthcare issues. Peter Graywater then told me that our employees have no idea on how good they have it at Packer Township and he wanted to hit somebody, preferably, Captain Kevin Dagg and Howard Goddard.

March 13
At the board meeting—Brandon Clinton and Pyle Goddard (past employees of the fire protection district) read scripted responses to the current issues. These individuals are past employees and threatened Peter Graywater, the board of trustees, and me. Clinton, Goddard, Captain Kevin Dagg, Richard Brice, and the other union members, invited the television and print media to be at this meeting so they can publicly humiliate me and to inform the public how bad the fire protection district is under my command.

March 14
This afternoon, Arthur Bode came into talk to me—he started by saying that he did not know what to say. I told him do not say anything. He told me that I have a lot of support in the township, and his mother really likes me.

Peter Graywater stopped by to tell me (reiterating) what Pyle Goddard said last night at the board meeting. He noted how Brandon Clinton threatened the board, him, and me. He also told me that after the executive session, the board left quickly to avoid the media and press.

March 17
Peter Graywater came into my office area and asked how my wife is doing. I said not well—he then said he wished he could do something about that, as he wanted to comfort her. Peter Graywater then asked if I would be interested in doing an interview with [a] TV channel— tell them your side of the story. I said no, not at this time. This is in accordance with my attorney's wishes.

Robert Burger, the planning and zoning czar, later came into my office area and told me that the executive session from last week's board meeting was to accept Frank Lynn's resignation effective the end of March and rehire him on the first of April so he can collect a paycheck and retirement—hence, double dipping.

March 19

Peter Graywater came into my office area. I had sent him some information via e-mail about the recent rainstorm and what the county had sent me on declaring area emergency zones. I then asked him if he wanted to go over the budget and he said, *"He did not have time that he had to deal with his fire chief getting into trouble."*

Today, at 11:06 a.m., Frank Lynn came into my office area and asked me if I resigned—I said no, and then he asked me if I was going to resign—I said NO. He then told me that [a] TV reporter called and said they heard a rumor. (This behavior is typical of fire department union militants.)

About 11:25 a.m., Peter Graywater asked me to come into his office. He asked me if I resigned—I said NO—and then asked if I was going to resign—I said no. He told me that the TV channel called and said that she got a call from an unknown caller that I had resigned. He then offered me to stay in his office while he called the TV channel back. Peter Graywater told the TV channel that I did not resign and that was only a rumor.

Peter Graywater then talked about the behavior of these people and I told him that the last time this happened; they placed an ad for my job in the fire chief association website. Peter Graywater then told me I had better not resign, and I told him I have no intention of resigning. Later in the afternoon, Lynn sent me a voicemail from Aaron Watt (former employee) asking for a copy of Chief Kelly Daugherty's current and past allegations—for his records.

March 25

Today about 2:00 p.m., Frank Lynn stopped by my office and asked me to go to Peter Graywater's office. When I arrived, Peter Graywater told me that the local newspaper said that they heard that there was a lawsuit filed—unknown whom against. I told Peter Graywater that I did not file any lawsuit. Peter Graywater contacted the Richmond County Prosecutor's Office and he said that there was no lawsuit against Packer Township or Chief Kelly Daugherty.

Around 4:30, Peter Graywater asked me to come to his office; he had received three phone calls—different reporters from the local TV channels stating that they received multiple calls stating that I resigned. Graywater called one of the reporters back and stated that I had not resigned.

Graywater also told me that a township resident is very upset over what the Packer Township firefighters are trying to do to me. *Peter Graywater also stated to me that "If you fucked up—you're gone; if you did not—you'll stay."*

I told Peter Graywater and Frank Lynn I have no intention of resigning. Frank Lynn starting kidding me about resigning and not letting him or Peter Graywater know. I told Peter Graywater that when I go to the YMCA to work out at night, people there tell me to hang in there. Peter Graywater also got a phone call from a past irate employee wanting a copy of the complaints.

Peter Graywater also told me that he is getting mad about people dragging HIS Packer Township's name through the mud. Peter Graywater also said that Harlow Rupp from the local newspaper was ordered to write a story—but after looking at my file, Peter Graywater said it looked like Harlow Rupp was disgusted he was doing this while saying that, "He did not want to do this" but "I have to do this." Throughout the entire story line, Harlow Rupp only reported one side of the story—the firefighters' lies side.

March 26

This morning, Peter Graywater accused me of padding the line item (other professional services) in the Fire District budget, saying it was, *"Big of me in the event that township was to fight me in court."* I told Peter Graywater that I was thinking ahead since this year was our labor/ management collective bargaining agreement renewal year and this was the only reason. Over the past two years, I budgeted $75K—this year, I budgeted $85K. This line item is also used for hiring personnel and background checks. We then went through other budget item issues, making sure everything was correct.

March 27

This afternoon, District Chief Baum and I were discussing going to the fire training update. District Chief Baum brought me a letter from Captain Patrick Jackson expressing his need to attend this meeting. District Chief Baum asked me to ask Frank Lynn and Peter Graywater if Captain Jackson can also go. I asked Peter Graywater about Captain Jackson's attendance and they said no. I did not see or look at the letter that Captain Jackson wrote, but District Chief Baum insisted on giving it to Peter Graywater, I said go ahead. District Chief Baum told Graywater that there would be consequences if Captain Jackson could not go. Peter Graywater later came to my office and told me that Captain Jackson made a threat to him—Peter Graywater also called Captain Jackson a *"cry baby"* not letting him get what he wanted.

In the evening, at the board meeting, Pyle Goddard got up to make comments about me but was told by Mr. Neil that the board will not take any comments about my status. He stated that they should not have let anyone say anything last meeting and that advice he said came from the township's attorney—the meeting ended.

April 1

This afternoon, I was talking with Frank Lynn about the water improvement project. He then asked me how I was doing. I told him I have good days and bad. He told me to "keep the faith," and I told him I always do. I also asked him how I should proceed about Craig Rider's evaluation. He told me that he and Peter Graywater were talking about that, that they would probably ask the board for an extension, and that he was going to talk to their township attorney about the matter.

The handbook does allow for a probation extension. However, if the board refused, the handbook states that the employee is terminated. Craig Rider had an unfavorable six-month review and a not-much-better nine-month review. Later I met with Peter Graywater about adding additional career personnel since one of our career employees was leaving for Iraq and we don't know if another career employee will be coming back after an off-duty injury. He said no—work the existing people with overtime.

April 2

Later this afternoon, Peter Graywater called me in his office to talk about some staffing issues. The conversation soon turned to how I am doing. I told Peter Graywater I meet with the Critical Incident Management Team (CISM) and go to exercise at the YMCA. A number of people stop by and say, "Hang in there, Chief."

A lot more people talk to my wife and say how tragic this situation is about what has happened to me and saying that they fully support me. I told Peter Graywater that just last Friday a neighbor stopped by to offer money to me for my defense fund. I told Peter Graywater I am amazed on how many citizens support me.

Peter Graywater started talking about the firefighters, identifying how negative they are. *He also said that the Packer Township firefighters are a "piece of work."* He then asked me if being at the government center isn't too bad. I said no, I am able to get quite a few things accomplished here. *He then said, "Well, you will need to be down at the fire house to keep those babies in line."* I did not say a word.

April 3

This morning, Mr. Robert Snow, our recently retired financial clerk, came to my office and told me to hang in there. He said he had the same thing happen to him thirty years ago, and he knows what type of person I am. This afternoon, Frank Lynn came in my office and asked me if we should keep Craig Rider or let him go. He also asked me if there had been improvement in Craig Rider. I told Lynn that Craig Rider is arrogant, argumentative, lacks interpersonal dynamic skills for the job, and I cannot trust him.

Craig Rider has not been on many major events in our area, and his ability to demonstrate his skills are vague. Frank Lynn told me that Peter Graywater wants to extend his probation, and I asked what that would do since he could not demonstrate his skills by this time. Frank Lynn again asked me if we should keep Craig Rider or let him go. I said let him go.

Lynn also asked me about Carl Eastman. Carl has been off work since Thanksgiving on an off-duty injury. I told Frank Lynn that Carl, when he first started, was good employee for our organization, but since then has not been much of a team player. Frank Lynn told me that he was going to talk to the township attorney on Friday on what they should do about both individuals.

April 4

This morning, I was talking to Frank Lynn about the firefighters killed in Shelby Township, and he told me that the information he has received (based on Chief John Prewer's investigations) over these allegations are all petty. He then said the firefighters do not know how good they have it here. Frank Lynn said that these firefighters say that I am a taskmaster, make them work too hard and train too much. He also said they like to sit around and do nothing.

Friday, April 4th, the Township of Shelby suffered a terrible blow [when] two firefighters died in a morning house fire. When I worked for the Shelby Township Fire Department, I was one of the training officers. I took this news very hard and could not believe the behavior of the Packer Township firefighters. I told Frank Lynn that a line-of-duty death is a fire chief's nightmare. I do my best to provide them with the best equipment, the best training, and promote team effectiveness. *Frank Lynn then said that the firefighters like to ride around in a $500,000 fire truck and visit the local restaurants.*

April 8

This afternoon around 2:30 PM, Peter Graywater came into my office asking what I had for the board Meeting—I had two items. He started talking about the firefighters saying that they are *"spoiled little princesses"* and that they don't recognize that the pendulum swings both ways. Per Peter Graywater, I was the only person authorized to attend the Shelby Township firefighters' funeral.

April 10

When I got to work, Peter Graywater asked me if any of our baby firefighters were at the funeral. I said yes.

This after the firefighters were told that I would be there representing the fire department, Fey Purdy, the fire district clerk, sent an email to Peter Graywater stating that Chief Dougherty should be in street clothes and the firefighters should had been able to attend the funeral. Graywater sent a reply e-mail stating that Fey Purdy was out of line.

From: Fey Purdy, Clerk
To: Peter Graywater
Subject: Funeral

Good Morning Peter

I can't believe the decision to let Chief Kelly Daugherty represent the Fire Protection District at the funeral of the fallen firefighters. Why are the rest of the firefighters from Packer Township being punished and not allowed to attend and represent the district they protect?

Something is very wrong here!!! Chief Dougherty should attend in street clothes not everyone else. I may be stepping out of place with this, but I just had to let you know that I don't agree with the decision!

From: Peter Graywater
To: Fey Purdy
Subject: RE: Funeral
Mrs. Purdy

You are stepping out of line. This was not a new decision. When I reassigned Chief Kelly Daugherty, my purpose was to separate the parties involved in a dispute. I do not intent to revisit the merit of that decision any time it doesn't suit someone's fancy whether that someone is Chief Kelly Daugherty or the Department. Therefore, Chief Kelly Daugherty WILL represent the Fire Protection District and you need to learn how to address me appropriately. Conversely, fire district personnel will not be showing up at events where it is most appropriate for the Chief to be the representative. The situation demanded a decision from the Administrator, I made it until the situation changes I don't intend to revisit because it is inconvenient or perceived as unfair by some individuals.

At the board meeting this same night, Pyle Goddard got up to talk, telling the board president that he should be allowed to talk about anything, even talk about the president's underwear. President Clark Neil kept saying, "What's your point?" At the end of the board meeting, an executive session was called for by Arthur Bode.

During the executive session, Police Chief John Prewer took one of the past employees around the building to talk to her about her negative behavior. At the beginning of the board meeting, a local resident overheard this person ask Pyle Goddard where Brandon Clinton was.

Apparently their little team of thieves did not all show up. The board meeting ended with no action.

April 11

This morning, I was speaking with Peter Graywater, trying to understand where Pyle Goddard was coming from when he addressed the board last night.

This afternoon, 4:15 p.m., Peter Graywater came into my office and told me, "Just so you know, the board is writing an apology letter to the fire district for not letting them go to the funeral last week." *Peter Graywater then said that he received a written reprimand in not letting the firefighters attend the funeral. When I asked for a copy of this reprimand, the township fiscal and records officer said that the document is not available. I told her in writing that I am making a public records request for this document. She failed to provide me the document, in violation of public records law.*

April 17

At 10:00 this morning—Craig Rider was with Frank Lynn for an hour and fifteen minutes. This afternoon, Frank Lynn said that Craig Rider was complaining because he had been "random" drug screened three times since he started working with Packer Township. I have no authority in deciding who receives notice to perform a drug test—this is all random and selected by our healthcare provider. Frank Lynn's has been very arrogant to me and short in his conversations.

Today, we had a structure fire and Engine 2 (with Captain Dale Mckee in command) lost its entire hose load (2,000 feet of five-inch hose) on the way to the run. Ladder 1 (with Richard Brice as the operator) wrecked the ladder truck into Medic 22 behind the station. Captain Dale Mckee immediately blamed Chief Daugherty for the hose bed issue since it did not have a tarp on the hose bed. (How narrow-minded can a person be?)

April 18

This afternoon, I received a complaint from a woman who says she was harassed and [subsequently] cited by Captain James Pickings and the City of Throop PD. I went into Peter Graywater's office and asked him to come to my office to hear the complaint she left on the answering machine. Her message says that Captain James Pickings targeted her for parking in the fire lane while she was restocking her business, while other cars in the other fire lane were let go.

Peter Graywater told me to have District Chief Michael Baum investigate the complaint right away. Meanwhile, her husband came to the government center to complain about Captain James Pickings' behavior. Frank Lynn had the husband go see Assistant Chief Craig Rider at the fire station. She also said she was going to the city building to complain.

After listening to the woman's complaint, Peter Graywater closed the door to my office and told me that he got a phone call from Ethel Meyer, reporter for the City of Throop newspaper. She told Peter Graywater that she had been to the station a number of times and she can see a difference on how people conduct themselves saying that since the *"leader is away, the mice are playing around."*

Peter Graywater also told me that he was being disciplined by the Board for not letting people to the funeral last week and that the Board is placing an apology letter in everyone's check next week. Peter Graywater said that the township thinks there is a pervert at the fire department but does not know who it is.

Peter Graywater also complimented me on how well I was holding up. I told him that I was hurting inside. He said it does not show and actually hugged me for staying strong and holding up under strong pressure. Frank Lynn told me that he has Assistant Chief Craig Rider talking to the complainant's husband, since he is next in command. The husband apparently was told by Frank Lynn to see Assistant Chief Rider at the firehouse this afternoon.

April 21

This morning after our safety meeting with Police Chief John Prewer and Frank Lynn, Frank said he wanted to talk to me about Assistant Chief Craig Rider. Frank Lynn told me that they wanted to extend Assistant Chief Craig Rider's probation, but our guidelines prohibit this. Frank Lynn also told me that if they let Assistant Chief Craig Rider go, he would have a claim against the township, so Frank Lynn wanted me to write up some positive things about Assistant Chief Craig. I said I could not lie; I am not like the other firefighters.

I do my job—do it well and am accountable for my actions. They do not and are not. Peter Graywater then came into Frank Lynn's office and told me that he was not about to get into any more tangled messes. I told Peter Graywater and Frank Lynn that I had written down issues regarding Assistant Chief Craig Rider and have them at home. Peter Graywater told me to go get them, so I did. When I returned, I provided Peter Graywater with two full pages of behavior issues I observed about Assistant Chief Craig Rider. Peter Graywater read them and told me that he would add this information to the board but would still recommend accepting Assistant Chief Craig Rider on a full-time basis.

April 23

Around 8:30 a.m., Peter Graywater arrived at work, and we began talking about our proposed website. He told me that he wanted to make sure that no one outside Packer Township employees sees the website yet, since it is not ready. *Peter Graywater then said that he "doesn't trust anyone at the fire department."*

Around 10:00 a.m., Police Chief John Prewer asked me if I had a moment. I said yes. He told me that he would interview me next week regarding the allegations to wrap things up. He told me he had interviewed the people he wanted to interview. I asked him what day and time since I needed to notify my attorney.

He said he would let me know by the end of the week. Around 11:00, I talked to Representative Susan Osborn from the blood bank. She asked me how I was doing. I told her one of the allegations we're in reference to the blood drive. *She was taken aback by this, saying that I am a person of high integrity, and she had never received any complaints about me.*

April 24

This is the letter that was sent out to the Packer Township firefighters regarding the on-duty fire-related deaths.

To: All Members and Staff of the Packer Township Fire Protection District:
Re: Firefighter Funeral Service

We recognize the brotherhood of firefighters and police officers and the importance of attending services for fallen brothers and sisters. We understand that some Packer Township Fire Protection District firefighters were not permitted to represent the Township at the recent services for the Shelby Township firefighters who passed away in the line of duty. While we recognize the unique circumstances that placed Township management in a difficult position when making this decision, upon further consideration we believe that a different course of action may have been more appropriate. We have taken steps to revise the Township's procedures for determining representation in similar future circumstances

Sincerely,
The Board of Packer Township Trustees

April 25

This morning while I was in Frank Lynn's office, he told me that last night's executive session with the board did not go as planned. He told me that he wanted to extend Assistant Chief Craig Rider's probation, but the board—under the advice of Lawrence Gray—said to take him off probation and give him his raise.

Frank Lynn also let me see Assistant Chief Craig Rider's evaluation, which has a number of *"below expectations."* Frank Lynn said he has not slept since this whole thing started and is amazed at how I am holding up. Frank Lynn also said that the board wanted to end the investigation, but that he told the board, "No, we need to interview Chief Kelly Daugherty yet."

April 29

Around 10:15 today, I talked with my attorney, Thomas Murtaugh, and he told me that the township attorney contacted his partner, Carl Peterson, asking if they could do a second investigation. Thomas Murtaugh told me that it appears that the township attorneys do not know what they are doing. Thomas Murtaugh also said it is time to send the letter to the administrator, Peter Graywater.

May 6

Today about 4:30, Police Chief John Prewer came into my work area and showed me a document. He asked me if this complaint resolution form was the one in existence back in 2003. I told Police Chief John Prewer that without placing them both side by side, I couldn't be sure, but that I believed it was the same document. I explained to Police Chief John

Prewer that we revise the fire district's standard operating procedures every three years, when the township revises the handbook. Police Chief John Prewer then asked me if I had labor management meeting minutes as far back as 2003, I said yes. He then told me that he was going to send me an e-mail requesting a copy of the minutes. I explained that I would be out of the office tomorrow but would send him anything he requested.

May 8
This evening's board meeting brought Pyle Goddard to address the board, complaining that the letter they had written to the firefighters over the funeral of the two Shelby Township firefighters was inadequate—saying they got a sow's ear and they wanted a silk purse. Goddard had a copy of the board's letter.

The board of trustees then met briefly and announced that they are having another person investigate the allegations about Chief Kelly Daugherty. At the first board meeting, Board President Clark Neil said ONLY Police Chief John Prewer will conduct such investigation. As a politician, Clark Neil changed his mind, all to appease the firefighters.

May 9
My attorney and I met with Police Chief John Prewer today at 10:00 a.m., and the meeting lasted until 1:30. Police Chief John Prewer confirmed that the union was behind the allegations. He also added he had names of the people alleging the complaints.

After the meeting, around 4:30, Frank Lynn and Peter Graywater asked me how I felt. I told them that I answered the questions as honestly as I could. Peter Graywater said that he knew I would. Frank Lynn asked me if I was surprised by anything, and I told him yes, I am surprised in the shift captains. Frank Lynn agreed.

May 15
Today, Captain Dale McKee was given a written reprimand for dropping the hose off E-2. Frank Lynn asked me what the fire department process is for appeals. I told him the complaint resolution procedure. Frank Lynn also told me that the Township management does not recognize complaints unless the formal complaint resolution process is utilized. There is a ten-day limitation on complaints, which had passed. If this is

the case, then why did the Township agree to accept hearsay complaints from years ago?

May 19

Robert Cooney, our vendor service technician, serviced my vehicle today. In the afternoon, Robert Cooney was talking with Peter Graywater. Robert Cooney stated that things are not the same at the fire district without the chief's presence. Things are in disarray. Later, Frank Lynn asked me for Robert Cooney's phone number, indicating that he wanted Chief John Prewer to call Robert Cooney and get information that is more detailed.

May 20

Today, Frank Lynn told me that he had a meeting with Assistant Chief Craig Rider. Frank Lynn said Craig Rider does not wanted to be involved in Captain Dale McKee's complaint resolution. Frank Lynn also said Craig Rider would evade questions posed by Frank Lynn and often tried to change the subject. *Frank Lynn also said the "white shirts" (meaning the officers) want to wear the badge but not follow through when it comes to imposing the rules or discipline.*

May 22

This morning, Peter Graywater asked my how my wife is doing. He said he was concerned about her. He told me that I would be fine—just concerned about her. *About this time, Peter Graywater informed me that he was leaving his wife of ten years since he fell in love with one of the secretaries at the county administrator's office. Peter Graywater also stated that he found his new love and cannot live without her.* Talk about creditability and loyalty – it appears that Graywater would jump ship when things are going rough. What ever happen to making a commitment?

May 27

Frank Lynn came in my office in the afternoon and told me that the new investigator will interview seventeen people, and my interview was scheduled as well. I asked if my attorney can be present; he said he did not know.

May 29

Attorney Thomas Murtaugh and I met with the new investigator for an hour and a half. The new investigator asked me the same information Police Chief John Prewer did. Afterward, Attorney Thomas Murtaugh told me he did not know what to think.

May 30

In the late morning, Peter Graywater asked me again how my wife was doing. This time, I told him she is very upset. He reiterated to me that he was concerned about her, but that he knew that I would be fine.

June 2

This morning at our safety meeting, Frank Lynn asked Police Chief John Prewer to identify what color carpet he would like, since the township is going to replace carpet in the Government Center. He then asked me but also said it did not matter; you will be back at the firehouse by then.

Pyle Goddard stopped by the Government Center this morning and spoke with Police Chief John Prewer. He wanted to see Frank Lynn and get a copy of Chief Kelly Daugherty's investigation report. We were in our Monday morning meeting and Pyle Goddard waited for a while but then left on his motorcycle.

June 3

I visited Dr. Bohn for a check-up this morning and he told me he recently saw an Austin firefighter who said, "They were out to get Chief Daugherty." He also said they were ungrateful.

Around 3:00, Peter Graywater told me he was waiting for the new investigator's report, saying that this report was determining my fate.

Around 4:30, Peter Graywater came back into my office and said he was still waiting for the new investigator's report. He was anxious and was teasing me over the report findings.

June 5

In the afternoon, after talking to my attorney, Thomas Murtaugh, I met with Frank Lynn and Peter Graywater and told them I am going to retire. I no longer want my family to go through the pain and suffering the Packer Township firefighters and administrators have imposed.

Both Peter Graywater and Frank Lynn then said, "Thanks—now we have to deal with these people. Thanks for putting us in this situation." I realized that Administrator Peter Graywater did not want me to stay, since it appears that by being ethical and honest, I was a threat to him, the members of the board of trustees (who were worried that I would run for political office), and the firefighters, who simply could not be honest and true and to follow a code of ethics.

Later, Peter Graywater gave me the unauthorized fire helmet, previously purchased by past fire chief Thomas Vandyke as a memento. I told him I did not want it. Peter Graywater forced the helmet on to me saying, "This is least he could do."

> "The world is not fair, and often fools, cowards,
> liars and the selfish hide in high places."
> —Bryant H. McGill

It is clear to me that the Packer Township board of trustees, under the advisement of its attorneys, had not followed the statutory requirements of due process as explained under the law. Chief John Prewer concluded my innocence in his completed investigation. However, the board president, Clark Neil, knowing that I had not violated any policies, was not—in my opinion—acting in the best interest of the citizens of the township, and wanted to keep dragging me through investigation after investigation. This was the straw that broke the camel's back and I was not going to let this happen.

CHAPTER 12

Decision-Making Process

"Managers are people who do things right.
Leaders are people who do the right thing"
—Richmond Bennis, PhD

In making my decision on what I would do, I had to ask myself, "What level of trust and honesty lies in the Packer Township government?" You just read deception issues from the fire department, Administrator Peter Graywater, and Assistant Township Administrator Frank Lynn, and the elected officials.

Police Chief John Prewer was never told by Frank Lynn to investigate the acts of Pyle and Howard Goddard, so there were never any charges filed, even after I requested that they be investigated. One main simple question remains:

Are we losing our moral compass?

Fire Service Reputations are at Risk. The nation's fire service has long been held in justifiably high esteem. This reputation has been hard earned. The fire service is that "rock of stability" to which the public knows to turn during the upheaval of a crisis—be that crisis a dwelling fire, rescue, natural disaster, or medical emergency.

Fire service members daringly charge into those situations from which others flee. We render these services to a grateful nation. The public, be it those who have been aided directly by the fire service or all the others who have merely borne witness to fire service heroics on the nightly news, is thankful that we are here and ready to serve at their beck and call. Nevertheless, not all is well, for that, hard-earned respect is easily lost.

When you have a governmental management attitude that permits

its workers to lodge unsigned complaints, complaints with no merit, and long timeframes, you then have a recipe for disaster. What ever happened to loyalty, honor, and dignity? Have you no shame?

Anytime Administrator Peter Graywater called (or even e-mailed me), he wanted to know if my wife was all right. He would then say that he *had "found the light in Jesus in his new girlfriend."* What a hypocrite.

Many of the residents in the city of Throop and Packer Township question the creditability of the elected officials, the appointed officials, and the fire department personnel. Character and creditability is something you earn, and I had done just that. Here is what one of the citizens had to say regarding my character.

The Packer Township Trustees

Dear Sirs,

I have had the pleasure of living in this community since 1987, 13 years in the City of Throop, and since 2000, on Main Street. I believe in my heart that all members of a community should give back to their community because doing so will invariably make a community stronger.

For the past 15 years, I have chosen to give back to Packer Township and the City of Throop by volunteering my time with various Scouting units, because building character in the young boys of today can lead to strong citizens tomorrow. I have had the opportunity of knowing Chief Kelly Daugherty through my scouting activities ever since he took over as head of the Packer Township Fire Protection District.

From time to time, I have had the need to ask him for assistance and whether it was for a Cub Scout Den to visit the Firehouse, the use of the Firehouse for CPR and First Aid Training class or the help of both the Fire and EMS Squads to help stage a mock emergency drill as part of a Merit Badge exercise, the respond from Chief Kelly Daugherty has always been the same, an unqualified "How can we help?"

The Chief understands that by helping my young men he is also giving back to the citizens of our community and in the long-run making it stronger.

I have had the opportunity to examine the allegations be

made about Chief Kelly Daugherty and I must say that on the surface they seem to be rather frivolous but one point mentioned by the plaintiffs stand out. They mentioned an incident where Chief Kelly Daugherty "arrived on the scene and initiated a confrontation with form employees" where he stopped them from using Fire District EMS equipment. To my way of thinking, Chief Kelly Daugherty's actions in this instance are to be commended.

Non-employees of the Packer Township Fire Protection District have NO business using District equipment, and any employee who allows such usage deserves to be reprimanded. This potential for litigation in this particular instance seems extreme and it appears to me that Chief Kelly Daugherty was acting with the best of interest of the Squad and the Township in mind. In my opinion, the Chief should be commended for his actions, I guess that for me, a citizen, and someone who might one day be in need of the services of the Fire and EMS Squads. It comes down to a simple question. Are we, the people of Packer Township, better off now under the guidance of Chief Kelly Daugherty than we were before he took office?

I remember the Firehouse on West Street in the City of Throop and when the current Station was built. I have voted for each Fire Levy that has come along because I have seen the need as our two communities have grown over the last 20 years, and was very pleased when, under Chief Kelly Daugherty's guidance, we were able to build staff and equip two satellite stations in the Township.

I have every confidence in the men and women of the Packer Township Fire Protection District and most especially in their Chief, Kelly Daugherty. I have known Chief Daugherty for a long time, and I have only ever seen him act with the best interest of our communities. I only hope that you can also see him in this light.

If you ask yourselves 'Are we, the people of Packer Township, better off now under the guidance of Chief Kelly Daugherty than we were before he took office?' It is my hope that you offer him and unqualified 'Yes'.

Sincerely,
Michael Simmons

Packer Township Resident

As you might imagine, all of these accusations have played a heavy toll on my family, my friends, and me. I sought the assistance of the Critical Incident Stress Management team, which did a great job in helping me keep things into perspective.

Dr. Elaine Dupe, Licensed Psychologist
1010 West Straight Street
Richmond County
Summary of Individual Support

The information contained in this report is privileged and confidential, and should not be released without the express written permission of Chief Kelly Daugherty and Mrs. Daugherty. Efforts to protect this information from unlawful disclosure consistent with HIPAA regulations are the responsibility of those to whom it is disclosed.

It has been my pleasure to offer Critical Incident Stress Management (CISM) support to Chief and Mrs. Kelly Daugherty. They were referred to me after an incident involving allegations made by fire department/union members and an intrusion into their personal life by the media.

Upon presentation, Chief Kelly Daugherty described the situation and the impact of these events on his personal and professional life. He described allegations, arising after an incident involving a non-breathing patient at the firehouse, where he stopped unauthorized personnel from providing emergency medical interventions. He described the presentation of an unsigned complaint and the township response, which was essentially, relieved him of command.

We discussed the impact of the Township directive that placed him in an ill-defined, ambiguous isolation at the Township building, and that prohibited him from contacting anyone in the department except for District Chief Michael Baum, while an investigation of the unsigned, undocumented complaint began.

Chief Kelly Daugherty described frustration with the disregard for departmental procedure, clearly outlined in policy and procedure manuals in addressing the complaints. He described that his duties at work were interrupted with little explanation and without due process. Trusting that an investigation would clear up any confusion, Chief Kelly Daugherty agreed to the Township's requests.

The impact of his removal from active command and the resulting isolation from department members created significant distress. This distress became heightened in relation to issues of departmental attendance at the funeral of a Line of Duty Death of two known firefighters. Because of the constraints placed on the department and Chief Kelly Daugherty, full departmental participation at the funeral, as is customary, was prohibited.

This distress led Chief Kelly Daugherty to seek support from the CISM team.

Our early meetings involved assisting Chief Kelly Daugherty to deal with the effects of 'shunning' from the department, and to cope with the pressures of the ensuing investigation. From the beginning, Chief Kelly Daugherty was eager to have the allegations investigated, stating he know he had done nothing wrong, and had nothing to hide. He cooperated fully with Police Chief John Prewer in his investigation.

Chief and Mrs. Kelly Daugherty felt the stress of the investigation and the pressures he felt from the isolation deeply. The Daugherty family faces inordinate amounts of stress, feelings of betrayal from the fire department staff, township administrators, and trustees. Despite a consistent history of outstanding performance evaluation, because of these allegations, Chief Kelly Daugherty had to cope with an attitude of disregard for his eleven years dedicated services to the community of Packer Township, and a lack of recognition of his significant contribution to departmental development made over the years. These overwhelming stresses and distress felt within his family, led Chief Kelly Daugherty to resign his position.

Since that time, Chief Kelly Daugherty has been actively engaged in securing subsequent employment. I have witnessed his eager participation in the job search process, his diligent preparation of application materials and active engagement in the interview process. He has applied for positions all over the Country.

Time and time again, when prospective employers become aware of these allegations, despite Chief Kelly Daugherty's full exoneration and a complete lack of charges, they have withdrawn offers of employment. Chief Kelly Daugherty has repeatedly needed to cope with the disappointment of being rejected as a candidate after successfully completing final stages of the interview and assessment process.

These disappointments have resulted in significant stress and anxiety. The professional isolation and inability to pursue his chosen vocation have compounded feelings of distress. Chief Kelly Daugherty has been an active participant in the Fire Service for thirty years and a departmental executive for over 15 years.

He has dedicated himself to assisting firefighting professionals to further their professional and educational development. He is a lifelong learner, having achieved a Master's Degree in Fire Service Leadership and is doctoral candidate. Despite these challenges, the Daugherty family has dealt with stresses with equanimity and composure, and with a continued focus to seek employment the next professional assignment.

I am happy to provide the court with any information about efforts to cope with the stresses and challenges that have been necessary since these unsubstantiated allegations were presented and the impact of these events in the personal and professional lives of Chief and Mrs. Kelly Daugherty.

> *Dr. Elaine Dupe, Licensed Psychologist*
> *Private Practice Clinical Psychology*

There is something wrong in Packer Township with its elected officials. For years, Chairman Clark Neil sold the township employee's healthcare insurance. Can you say "conflict of interest"? According to the Richmond Register newspaper, a Richmond County judge recently appointed a special prosecutor to review the investigative report completed by the Ethics Commission on Chairman Clark Neil.

Chairman Clark Neil has been the subject of an ongoing ethics investigation for nearly fourteen months, based on findings against him in connection with about $1.2 million in health insurance coverage provided to Packer Township that was administered by his insurance agency. Private attorneys advised Packer Township that Neil's agency could administer the township's health insurance. However, the state audit, aided by the Packer Township fiscal officer, made a finding against Chairman Clark Neil involving two laws prohibiting public officials from gaining something of value and having unlawful interest in public contracts.

In a related article, the Packer Township fiscal officer stated it is time, after more than a year, for the commission to conclude its investigation of Chairman Clark Neil's insurance agency's role in administering the township's health insurance coverage.

The Packer Township handbook clearly states: "Representation by present or former public official or employee prohibited."

No present or former public official or employee shall, during public employment or service or for twelve months thereafter, represent a client or act in a representative capacity for any person on any matter in which the public official or employee personally participated as a public official or employee through decision, approval, disapproval, recommendation, the rendering of advice, investigation, or other substantial exercise of administrative discretion.

When Trustee Arthur Bode, Chairman Clark Neil, and Trustee Todd Lowe wanted us to solicit information for their re-election, that was a clear violation of the ethics law, which states:

No public official or employee shall solicit or accept anything of value that is of such a character as to manifest a substantial and improper influence upon the public official or employee with respect to that person's duties.

One must ask themselves the following questions:
   a) Does my company stand for something—anything—special?
   b) Am I excited to see my colleagues when I show up for work on Monday morning?
   c) Do I have a voice at work?
   d) Does anyone who matters listen to what I say?

I took this matter to a higher level in the judicial system and the results are more astounding than I had thought. The Common Pleas Court in Richmond County and the Appeals Court found that it is fine for firefighters to lie and not be held accountable for their actions. Based on their ruling, firefighters and supervisors of firefighters will not be held at a higher standard. It is permissible for them to ruin a person's livelihood and career.

Packer Township had accepted the position of blaming others and not being held accountable for their actions. When you have accusations and innuendo they say dates back over eight years, *with no proof,* this can only lead one to believe that Packer Township believed and practices that it is acceptable to bully, criticize, torment, and dehumanize a person for their own personal gain. This is unbelievable by any stretch of the imagination.

My decision to move on was not an easy one. I did a lot of introspection and made my decision on the following issues.

- Packer Township is more engrossed in appeasing people who do not do their jobs and are not accountable, so this must be a reflection of the organization as a whole. When the ship is sinking, you are allowed to bail.
- I believe in consistency and subscribing to a participatory style of management. I always seek input from various levels inside and outside the organization. Over the years, I have guided my management philosophy with both union and non-union employees. Having input from everyone ensures that I am listening to all relevant concerns and seeking plausible solutions from multiple perspectives. I actualize these values in my duties and responsibilities as an effective team leader, constantly looking for ways to improve the overall performance of the fire department .
- No single department carries the community's government mission single-handedly. Communications and the ability to work with others are essential in delivering vital township's services to our constituents. Collectively, we work best together—but apparently, it is all about egos.

While I thought I had a good relationship with the township management and the elected officials, I had no idea that their goal was to have me eliminated. In turn, this clearly is a hostile work environment.

My personal thoughts and values no longer are in line with the Packer Township culture. As fire chief, I am a visible township leader. The role is synonymous with integrity, honesty, and having high-quality communications skills. The fire chief is the principal agent, overseeing the day-to-day operations, and must have exemplary visionary and networking skills.

As such, as the fire chief, I am a leader, mentor, coach, and manager with the ability to interact with the various individuals and departments. I seek ways to work in harmony for the stakeholders. Peter Graywater did not approve of me working with state and local committees on issues that affect our service, which really is counterproductive to being a good leader.

The Packer Township managers and elected officials appear to engage in questionable business practices. When you have a board president selling health care insurance to over one hundred township employees—one would think that there is clearly a conflict of interest.

My requests for continually improving the Fire Protection District were being ignored and unappreciated. On a number of occasions, my requests for fire service-related personnel, equipment, and policies were all ignored by Peter Graywater. In fact, at one of my last staff meetings, *Peter Graywater told me, "Never ask for anything—you got all you need to do the job."*

I always took into account any unexpected issues that may arise throughout the course of the year. I am proud to say that over the past eleven years as fire chief, even with increased demands by our firefighters to spend more, I was able to keep the fire department operating budget balanced and accurate, meeting both the township's and organization's expectations.

My hard work and job security is now being threatened. When Frank Lynn reminds me that I am "already retired" (just because I am utilizing a benefit that the law allows), then there is a serious personality disorder on Frank Lynn's part.

Finally, the belief that I—a seasoned veteran of public safety with a stellar work record—would ever engage in any inappropriate activity is simply unbelievable. I thought the township officials believed in me, but I guess not. My leadership and management style is straightforward; I set the example. I require that effective controls are developed and maintained to ensure the integrity of the fire department . While I believe that empowerment within an organization is important, I do hold all supervisors accountable for carrying out the department rules and responsibilities.

I have developed an accountability involvement model, which ensures accountability from each fire department officer, designed to maintain operational readiness throughout the organization. You can rely on me to ensure that projects are complete, delivered in a timely manner, and within budget. I make it a point to monitor and evaluate plans and projects, focusing on quantifiable results.

How can you expect others to lead by example when the administrator, Peter Graywater and other elected officials fail to uphold the law and do the right thing? It was apparent that the Packer Township and City of Throop leadership would rather take advantage of people than to tell them the truth. This is where I draw the line. Their beliefs do not fit my beliefs, therefore I have a choice—and I chose not to be part of their scheme any longer.

I interviewed for over one hundred fire-service positions since that time, and I still recall one village manager asking me about the credentials of Peter Graywater and Frank Lynn.

"Are they International City Manager Association certified?" this person asked.

I said they were not.

"Do they actively engage in the township?" he asked.

I said, "They sit behind their desks all day long."

He then said, "They have no credentials."

This made me think even harder about the Packer Township culture and environment.

I was, however, offered employment with the village, only to have it rescinded when the Packer Township professional firefighters called the village manager and the local press, telling them about how I treated them. Other city managers also told me that Packer Township professional firefighters called them as well. When they asked for the names, the person said, "We are Packer Township professional firefighters—and that is all you need to know."

Insights I received by family, friends, and colleagues made me realize that I no longer wish to be in the same workplace with Chairman Clark Neil, Gregg Lowe, Arthur Bode, Peter Graywater, and Frank Lynn, and their unethical and anomalistic behaviors.

Ethics is based on the recognition of certain human rights. An individual has the right not to be deliberately deceived. He has the right not to be forced to go against his conscience. He has the right to expect other parties to live up to their commitments and to behave according to the law.

In the workplace, the employer has the right to expect employees to behave according to company policy. This also means that everyone follows the rules, not just a few. In addition, just because you have ethical rules in some handbook that does not mean that people will follow them.

Saying good-bye to something you focused your career on is very difficult. I am an optimist—always looking at the glass half-full rather than half-empty. I put together a simple one-page resignation letter, expressing my appreciation for the opportunities afforded to me.

To: *Frank Lynn, Assistant Administrator/Safety Director*
From: *Kelly Daugherty, Fire Chief*
Subject: *Retirement*

I would like to inform you that I am retiring from my position as Fire Chief effective December 1, 2008.

The Packer Township Board of Trustees and Administrators had provided me the opportunity to lead, manage, and develop our fire district into the flagship of northern Richmond County, and I thank them for their support, mentoring, and guidance. I have enjoyed working for Packer Township and the City of Throop and appreciate the support provided me during my tenure.

*"Life isn't about waiting for the storm to pass…
it is learning to dance in the rain."*
—Unknown

Chapter 13
Do the Right Thing, Every Time

"I know God will not give me anything I can't handle.
I just wish that he didn't trust me so much."
—*Mother Teresa*

These firefighters have actively participated in a silent sabotage and acted as domestic terrorists—and Administrator Peter Graywater and elected officials of Packer Township permitted their behavior to prevail. Instilling fear may help one achieve a specific short-term goal but it is hardly the same as "exercising leadership." One who inspires, creates buy-in, creates a road map for achievement of common goals, builds an effective team, and assigns roles in keeping with capacity is leading. These folks have a lot to learn.

One who bullies, behaves arbitrarily, or otherwise instills fear is more likely to breed failure than success. Fearful people are often too timid in their decision-making or too stressed to analyze dispassionately, and that may well stir resentment that can lead to betrayal and silent sabotage. There has to be accountability, and people who do not perform may need to be replaced. However, the process, the standards, and the expectations should be clearly spelled out, and every effort should be made to ensure a successful performance. That, not instilling fear, is the true exercise of leadership.

One of the most impressive undertakings we engaged in is to have candidates participate in a psychological evaluation to determine their "mental" fitness for duty. In the world of emergency services, there are no time-outs, no halftime breaks, and no substitutions. As emergency service providers, you must have the physical and mental capacity and stamina to perform the job effectively.

In my opinion, some of these "professionals" simply are lacking the knowledge depth to understand how their actions affect the community at large. As such, cancerous cells expand, and if not controlled, they will take over the entire governmental body.

One of the questions I ask a potential candidate is, "If your neighbor, a person whom you had known since grade school, recently lost his/her job, and is having a hard time meeting financial obligations, suddenly is found with what may appear to be stolen items they are selling at their yard sale, would you report them to the police or keep this secret to yourself. It amazes me that every time I ask this question, the candidate says that they would do the right thing and report their unlawful actions to the authorities.

Yet, it is these individuals whom, for whatever reason, decided to join a cancerous bandwagon, and fabricate lies, hearsay, and innuendos with the appearance that someone else is the problem – not them. Most dictionaries agree that a conspiracy is an inchoate, or preparatory, crime. It is similar to solicitation in that both crimes are committed by manifesting an intent to engage in a unlawful act. It differs from solicitation in that conspiracy requires an agreement between two or more persons, whereas solicitation can be committed by one person alone.

Leaders have a tremendous impact on the motivation of their people and the resulting productivity. While there are great debates on a leader's ability to motivate people, this course will operate under this premise: Leaders do not motivate people; they create an environment in which people choose to motivate themselves. When leaders reward certain types of behavior and performance and ignore others, they are telling their people what is important. This in turn will affect job performance and productivity.

Another factor that influences motivation and performance is the expectation of the leader. Most people will only do that which is expected of them. Some will struggle to even reach that level of performance, while peak performers will consistently exceed expectations set for the average worker. A leader generally gets what he or she expects. Therefore, it is critical to set high yet achievable expectations for themselves and their employees.

These expectations should vary from individual to individual to allow them to use their various strengths and improve on their weaknesses. While it is important to set the same minimal performance expectations for everyone doing the same job, a ten-year veteran firefighter should be challenged to do more than one still on probation.

I carry a servant leadership philosophy. The concept of servant leadership has recently become very popular, but it is not new. Good leaders naturally do good things and make their lives matter. Servant leaders do great things by serving others. They do not *tell* people what to do; rather they ask, "What can I do for you? What can I do to help you succeed at your job? What do you need from me?" Servant leadership is not easy for some supervisors to embrace, but it permits the greatest number of people to experience the greatest rewards.

It is the ultimate win-win relationship. The unfortunate part to this is I had worked very hard to gain buy-in from others, including funds from the public in the tune of 40 million dollars over ten years, to increase staffing, purchase new equipment, improve safety and training, and enhance wellness awareness, and the "professionals" still want more.

There is a well-known belief that is expressed in a variety of ways—one of the few things that remain constant in life is change. Compare that with another well-known fact: people do not like change, and they do not like to accept change. When those two statements are matched up, it is easy to see why so many people and organizations are experiencing so much turmoil. Advancements in technology, along with a variety of other factors, seem to have greatly accelerated change, and there are no signs of this stopping or even slowing down.

It is believed that a large percentage of the world's population resists change. They resist anything that changes their routines, attempts to move them outside their comfort zone, or makes them do more than they are accustomed to doing. This is why there is a typically a time lag in making change in a large organization (defined as one hundred or more people). Any significant change takes approximately three to five years.

Most of this is due to psychological and sociological factors that form a strong basis for people's resistance to change. This explains why the culture of a police or fire department is so difficult to change and why city leaders looking for change bring in a police or fire chief from the outside. Even with a change at the top of the organization, changing the culture of an organization takes several years. The larger the agency, the more steeped in tradition, the harder, and longer it will be before change takes effect. In changing a culture, leaders must establish their philosophy early on, believe in themselves, then stay the course.

Leaders search for opportunities to change the status quo. They look for innovative ways to improve their organizations. They experiment and take risks, and because risk-taking involves mistakes and failure, leaders accept the inevitable disappointments as learning opportunities. Most organizations discourage people from challenging the status quo or from making waves.

Fire-service organizations are especially guilty of this. Their emphasis is on following the rules, obeying the organization's policies and procedures, and *staying within the lines*. Challenging the process or confronting peers and superiors with different ideas is viewed as the behaviors of someone who is not a team player.

In my opinion, surrendering your moral ethics has consequences. Moral principles create ethical boundaries by which people live. Without them, society would be in chaos. A code of ethics defines a person's identity and decency. Life becomes worthy of being lived when a person is capable of remaining true to his morals. What is more, during times of trial a person's morality is tested.

When that person overcomes the adversity, while staying true to his moral values, true courage, and character shine through the shadows of wickedness. Furthermore, the behavior of an individual, especially in times of trouble, is a direct result of that person's moral principles.

As I walked through this journey, a few plausible explanations, besides the ones identified, came to light. They include:

- This was a union negotiation year. The union wanted more power and control and management was steadfast in maintaining control.
- Captain James Pickings wanted more money, wanted to have different bugle insignias on his shirt to make him different and separate him from the other captains, more prestige, and wants the career personnel to do more inspections.
- Captain James Pickings is upset over a recent pay raise, feels that I am not supporting him, and does not want to perform duty-officer responsibilities without additional pay. Captain James Pickings has wanted a 24/48 schedule for himself so he can make more money. As a salaried employee, they do not get overtime and Captain James Pickings wants to do this only to get more money.
- Captain James Pickings tried for the assistant chief position

twice and has not been promoted, and holds that against the chief. Captain Pickings has become very bitter toward me, and I believe he is using this forum to get his revenge.

- For more than three years, I addressed a serious water-flow deficiency in the southern part of the community. I have been trying to get the stakeholders to build a water tower able to protect the surroundings, should a petroleum line or tank rupture and catch fire at the bulk fuel terminal; however, Captain Pickings was wanting the glory and prestige and did not want to perform the research to justify such request.

Richmond County Administrator Ely Wall told me that after hearing of what Captain James Pickings and the Packer Township Professional Firefighters had done to me, he recommended that the "Richmond County Commissioners "cut the funding mechanism" for this project. The Richmond County Commissioners were willing to pay the $6 million dollars and have the petroleum companies occupying the hazardous area pay the county back within twenty years.

- Patrick Jackson does not want to feel belittled and is disturbed that Frank Lynn wants him to do the District of Worker's Compensation paperwork for the entire township employee base. Patrick Jackson often complains that he has to do accident investigations, gets upset when training priorities change from time to time, and like Captain James Pickings, wants to be treated as a chief officer.
- Richard Brice has issues with Peter Graywater and Frank Lynn over sick bank policy—wanting more time for "his people." Richard Brice wants more for his union personnel, wants more career people in general. Richard Brice would often cry if we did not have one hundred candidates competing for a career position. Richard Brice had a high life change—had to get married, entered an existing family of three, fighting for Carl Eastman (who is off on off-duty medical leave) to have the township start a sick bank program.

- The Fire Protection District, with the inflows of new lieutenants, is going through growing pains, this coupled with Assistant Chief Craig Rider who is confrontational with our organizational system. Assistant Chief Craig Rider tries to be more of a buddy than a boss for the firefighters. He even asked Police Chief John Prewer, "Off the record, if Chief Kelly Daugherty retires today, would this just go away, would it just stop here?"

Prewer's response was, "I would not be asking the chief to retire, and he has the right to fight the complaints against him." The question was asked in an interesting way, as if it was to hint to have someone ask the chief to retire.

- The Packer Township board of trustees awarded me an unexpected 6 percent raise, while the non-contract employees received a 4 percent raise, and the contract employees received (by contract) a 3 percent raise this past year.
- With the latest lieutenant promotions, the union now knows that there will not be any more promotional opportunities. The last two candidates are from outside the department.
- Captain Kevin Dagg wanted to keep Pyle Goddard as his friend. He also has been pestering me to let him be the first shift commander, with a staff vehicle, so he can be in charge at fires. Kevin Dagg wants to be the "big man on campus" but is not willing to take the responsibility.
- The union, through Richard Brice, has often expressed displeasure in our current labor management contract—stating that management has too many options, and they do not like it when they ask for something and I say no. The management-rights issue in the contract is not going to change.
- Outside of the department, persons who have an issue with me are past employees including Pyle and Howard Goddard. Howard Goddard is a lieutenant with a neighboring fire department, and while he has talked negatively about his father's behavior in the past, I believe he and Kevin Dagg

are behind getting our union in an uproar and letting our
union fight this fight.

> *"The circus tents may be a different color,*
> *but the clowns are all the same."*
> —George Carlin

A good friend of mine wrote a response to what I had encountered,
and I was not surprised that this type of behavior has occurred to other
Chief Fire Executives as well. This article, "Adverse to Vision," is from
Fire Chiefs magazine.

> *One of the more reprehensible things I have seen in recent
> years has been the damage done to chief officers' reputations by
> accusations from anonymous sources. These accusations have
> been sent to commissioners or Administrator Peter Graywater
> via letter or e-mail or through strategically placed rumors, and
> in at least two instances have marred very innovative chiefs with
> unfounded allegations against their character. In both of these
> cases, the chiefs turned marginal departments into progressive
> organizations, cutting dead wood as they evolved. While difficult
> to prove, these anonymous character assassinations seemed to
> follow instances where individuals were passed over or demoted
> for their failure to perform.*
>
> *In one instance where the wrongly accused chief decided
> to leave because of the lack of support he received from his
> commissioners, the Fire Protection District he oversaw reverted
> back into the two departments he had help consolidate. It has
> been several years since his decision to leave, and while one of
> the departments continued to progress under strong leadership,
> the other has struggled just to provide day-to-day operations
> and has had two catastrophic meltdowns following major fires
> in past years.*
>
> *In the most recent example of this type of adversity, a chief held
> on long enough to retire, leaving a legacy within his department of
> two new stations, a complete turnover of the fire and EMS fleet, a
> significant decrease in his district's response time, a set of written*

SOGs, as well as inspection and public-education programs that enhanced both citizen and firefighter safety.

Unfortunately, he may not be remembered for all the progress he brought to his Township, but rather for the unfounded accusations against him. Since his retirement, my friend has diligently sought another career in the fire service. He has hit these allegations head on by openly discussing them with potential employers and sharing copies of the two reports that exonerate him of all the alleged charges.

What has kept my friend going is the support he has received from within his network of fellow chiefs. Early on, he made it a point to reach out to a select circle of close friends for advice, and fortunately for him has received continued support and strength through this process. What I have learned is that despite the efforts of two of the finest chiefs I have known, sometimes the dark side of human nature turns those we are compelled to discipline into cowardly, vindictive individuals bent only on the destruction of our best and brightest.

Occasionally I remind myself that leadership requires understanding of why we have adversity and opposition to our vision. The truth is that the greater a leader's accomplishments, the greater the opposition or discouragement an adversary will attempt to throw at your plans. Their objective is to derail the progress or bring the chief down to their level. The trick is to expect and even anticipate this adversity and know that it is a sign that you as chief are actually doing the right thing for your organization. The best way both my friends and I have found in difficult situations is to surround ourselves with a network of true professionals whom we can call upon for frank, honest advice, and then carry through with our ideas while maintaining our professionalism and integrity.

A person works very hard over most of his career, treating people fairly, helping to build a better and safer community—and this is the way the Packer Township officials treat the person who led an organization to prosperity? Makes you wonder how many other managers, supervisors, directors, and chief executive officers, in both the private and public sectors, have been mistreated in a similar manner.

This unfortunate list of incidents needs to serve as an example for current and future supervisors. You never know the motives of others. What I do know is that if you are honest, seek opportunities, and are willing to go above the expectation, there is no guarantee that what happened to me would not happen to you; however, the experience you gain regarding human behavior is invaluable.

Therefore, as a manager, supervisor, chief executive officer, or someone having human resource responsibilities, my recommendation is to do the best job you can and be honest, dependable, and true. When faced with adversity, just remember to live with integrity and make a positive difference in doing the right thing.

CHAPTER 14
Ethical Challenge

"Keep integrity and your work ethics intact. So what if that means working a little harder; an honorable character is your best calling, and that's something anyone can have!"
—Kathy Ireland

According to the "Fire Service Reputation Management" white paper, the most basic concept of all that can help us understand these issues and begin to plan strategies to reduce the problems experienced in the fire service is also the most important concept: The fire service seems to be suffering from a crisis of ethics or lack of ethical integrity.

Some leaders have expressed a concern that this problem of integrity, or ethics, is partly the result of a fire service culture so burnished with the moniker of "hero" that its members ultimately forget that they must continually earn the public's trust. It is true that many firefighters have performed heroically. For this honorable and deserved commitment to public duty, the citizens of many communities have been steady in their support of the fire service.

"Have the courage to say no. Have the courage to face the truth. Do the right thing because it is right. There are the magic keys to living your life with integrity."
—W. Clement Stone

It is frightening when hearing Chief Prewers previous statement, "There was a complete failure on the part of Captains Kevin Dagg, Tracy Blackman, Dale McKee, James Pickings, and Patrick Jackson; Lieutenants Robert Story, Lloyd Whipple, Anthony Gibbs, Eric Brooks,

Gilbert Brown, Wayne Folsom; District Chief Michael Baum and Assistant Chief Craig Rider to do their jobs."

The antidote to a false sense of entitlement is to rebuild the fire service's foundation of ethical behavior and ethical decision-making. One step in that direction is to establish a national Fire Service Code of Ethics as a guide for improved ethical decision-making. From the establishment of an agreed-upon code of ethics, fire service ethical behavior can become part of the training every firefighter receives, from the beginning of basic recruit training to courses at the National Fire Academy, and then expanding into fire science higher education programs for future leaders.

As a start, the "Fire Service Reputation Management" white paper seeks to increase the awareness of the fire service about the ethical foundations of our public service. Each of the fire service reputation management issues addressed should give the reader pause for thought in three areas, a) individual decisions that can cross the line of acceptability in the minds of the public, b) leadership responsibility to understand the ways to minimize the harm from these types of incidents, and c) the opportunities to clarify the ethical basis supporting the fire service mission locally and nationally.

It is important to understand that ethical challenges permeate our daily lives. It may be as simple as the vehicle repair bill that did not include filling up the windshield washer reservoir. It may be as complex as contractual conflicts of interest coupled with brutal political battles in a large government agency. The ethical challenge knows no scope. It only knows outcome.

Are our choices clear? When was the last time you faced an ethical dilemma? It may not have been a life-or-death issue, but just something that shook the arrow on your ethical compass. Were those involved in these situations acting with malicious intent? Were overzealous employees attempting to gain an edge or cut corners? As our stock falls, so does our moral currency. However, we can modify behavior by looking back at past behavioral beliefs.

Past ethical teachings help us remain within the ethical boundaries. They include:

a) Immanuel Kant's Means/Ends Rule: A person is not to be used as a means to another person's end.

b) Fairness (Golden Rule): Do unto others, as you would have them do unto you.

c) Fairness (Platinum Rule): Treat others as they wish to be treated.

d) Kant's Categorical Imperative: Only perform those acts which you would allow to become universal standards.

e) Professional Ethics Rule: Is this standard behavior for your peers?

f) Utilitarian Rule: The greatest good is whatever brings the greatest good to the greatest number of people.

The fire service faces a host of issues that threaten its integrity and sterling public image. This risk is increased by the lightning speed at which information, and sometimes misinformation, is transmitted and propagated. Moreover, because of the continuing advent of technology, no longer can any issue be considered truly "local" as even the most isolated of matters affecting the most far-flung of departments can sully the reputation of the entire fires service.

Some of the issues discussed herein are not new. Recognizing that the actions of a small minority of bad actors can have grievous widespread consequences, the fire service as a whole must be increasingly vigilant in policing itself. Through a combination of enhanced and improved internal controls, increased vigilance, and greater acceptance of personal responsibility perhaps including, a Code of Ethics, the fire service can ensure that it remains true to its roots and heritage of protecting and serving this great nation.

To preserve the public's trust, a National Firefighter Code of Ethics was developed by a group of fire service leaders that calls on individual firefighters to pledge their support for maintaining the highest level of professionalism and behavior.

The Code of Ethics serves to remind our firefighters and other public safety providers of our moral and ethical obligation to the profession as well as to the people we serve. The public places great trust in our profession, and we need to exercise good judgment in order to preserve that trust.

The ethical challenge I submit to you contains three distinctive components:

1. Seek out these destructive, vicious, and negative individuals,

eliminate all forms of deceit, and replace them with integrity-minded individuals.

2. Consider taking the Firefighter Ethical Challenge at *www.firefighterbehavior.com*.
3. Be true to yourself, your family, your friends and share your ethical values with others.

Only then can we honestly have heroes who are honest, optimistic, and devoted, who practice humility and exhibit high moral character, and are able to perform this essential safety-sensitive work with the right intentions.

> *"The most important persuasion tool you can have in your entire arsenal is integrity."*
> —*Zig Ziglar*

About the Author

Chief Kelly Daugherty began his fire service career in 1975 as a part-time/volunteer firefighter/EMT with the Shelby Township Fire Department. He was promoted to a career position in 1978. He worked through the ranks, obtaining positions as a fire apparatus operator, aerial tower operator, advanced EMT, shift lieutenant, and fire captain. In 1996, Chief Kelly Daugherty accepted the position of assistant chief with the Williamson Fire Department, and in 1999, accepted the position of fire chief for the Packer Township Fire Protection District.

Chief Daugherty has extensive experience in fire, emergency medical service (EMS), and emergency management and is active in various professional associations. Chief Daugherty is the past state fire director, past economic committee chairman, past member of the Richmond County Local Emergency Planning Commission, and a five-term past vice president of the Richmond County Fire Chiefs Association.

Kelly Daugherty earned a bachelor of science degree in fire and safety engineering technology, a master of science degree in public safety leadership; is a graduate of the National Fire Academy's Executive Fire Officer Program (EFO); and is certified as a Chief Fire Officer Designate (CFO) from the Centers for Public Safety Excellence.